THE ORGANIC SOCIETY

THE ORGANIC SOCIETY

Carlos Sosa Araque

Library of Congress Control Number:		2017904566
ISBN:	Hardcover	978-1-5065-1973-9
	Softcover	978-1-5065-1972-2
	eBook	978-1-5065-1971-5

Print information available on the last page.

Rev. date: 30/03/2017

To order additional copies of this book, contact:
Palibrio
1663 Liberty Drive
Suite 200
Bloomington, IN 47403
Toll Free from the U.S.A 877.407.5847
Toll Free from Mexico 01.800.288.2243
Toll Free from Spain 900.866.949
From other International locations +1.812.671.9757
Fax: 01.812.355.1576
orders@palibrio.com
759810

"There is an old mistery in the universe:
Why life?
What is Creation for?
Intelects seek for and search
unsuccessfully;
They invent theories,
but the ancient mystery
only reveals itself to love,
to the consciousness illuminated by love.
A privilege of those who are simple and
uncomplicated, like children".

(Introduction to the Pergamin of the old Krato,
inhabitant of planet Kia, in "Amy Returns"
by Enrique Barrios)

DEDICATION

To Love,
That magnificent force that takes us by the hand
through mysterious paths of Life

CONTENTS

ACKNOWLEDGEMENTS

Thanks to my family, Andreina, Alexander and Gabriela, for teaching me every day how to love and be loved.

Thanks to Paulo Reis for reading and providing his feedback many years ago.

Thanks to Melissa Navas for her assistance in proofreading the text.

Thanks to Fanny Hadjis for her support in translating the first pages.

Thanks to Leonardo Faccini for giving me the idea of translating this book.

Thanks to our spiritual guides for providing us with continuous support in the paths of life.

INTRODUCTION

Modern institutions are characterized for having been designed under the mechanicist organizational model. Bureaucratic structures, hierarchies, the instrumental character of individuals, the organization's segmentation in multiple parts, the functionalist character of relationships among the parties, as well as the tailoring of means towards the achievement of objectives form part of a way of thinking inspired by the Cartesian rationality, and is expressed as the bureocratic-mechanicistic organization.

This type of structure exhibits a series of characteristics that prove ineffective for our current times, as is the lack of flexibility and proper adaptation to mutable environments. On the other hand, the bureocratic-mechanicistic structure shows implicit deficiencies to appropriately deal with the sources of motivation of man, in light of which several proposals have arisen throughout this century, inspired by theories of humane nature that seek to motivate man within the working environment. The results of these initiatives though, have led far from meeting the expectations created.

In parallel, Modern Society is determined by a rational economic system, based on the individualistic behavior of man, which determines and models social institutions, yielding thus as a result a great extent of material riches and technological progress, where the elements associated to equality and solidarity, however, are not properly incorporated into the economic systems. This induces a constant global economic growth without taking into consideratiom its viability in the long-term, obeying to facts such as the marginalization of large population sectors, the uneven distribution of riches, the extinguishment of resources, the unstable flow of speculative capitals, the alienation of individuals and the environment's pollution.

Both the bureocratic-mechanicistic structure and the market system originate from the rational analysis of reality. Rationality, a symbol that belongs by excellence to the Modern Age, has reduced the analysis of society and mankind to the level of mechanical systems. The rational paradigm allows seeing reality as an inmense machine, leaving aside a series of factors inherent to their organic nature. All systems are treated as machines: the elements composing it are separated, analyzed and synthesized, failing to establish the difference between the set of elements functioning separatelly and the system as a whole.

Despite this reality, organizations, social systems and society in general can be seen from a different standpoint. These can be analyzed as a large quilt of overlapping relations, with additional priorities to the sum of its parts, where the conceptual metaphor are not machines but the organic structure, inspired by the natural organic systems. Organic structure is understood as the type of organizational and social structure based on the model provided by organic systems. In this type of structure, man's consciousness will play a paramount role, as his successful integration will depend on the harmonious behavior of the individuals forming part of this structure, and the permanent quest to achieve balance between the personal and collective wellbeing.

In addition, we deem necessary exploring other dimensions of human reality other than rationality, in order to accomplish our true purpose: the implementation of a type of organization that uses the organic metaphor as source of inspiration for a more harmonious social reality. To this end, we must resort to a series of factors inherent to the human nature, that reflect, in one way or another in the organizational reality, such as a sense of consciousness, solidarity and *Love*.

Seems quite paradoxical the fact that we must resort to rational arguments, through written words in this essay to introduce elements other than rationality to include additional factors that have an influence in the behavior of man. Love, consciousness, solidarity and other non-rational arguments can only be transmitted in rational terms thanks to the use of the written word, based on what they can project in the rational plane; even if we acknowledge that we will never be able to explain or depict accurately these facets of the human experience in rational terms. Using a graphic metaphor, just as the cube can only be explained in bi-dimensionality terms as a square, the same happens in trying to explain some non-rational aspects of life in rational terms in a text, through their projection in the rational plane and the use of language, with the inherent limitations implied therein. However, given the need to convey such arguments, we accept the use of language in order to try to explain that there is another kind of language that would allow us understanding better the human dimension. In some segments, this essay will be severe with the reader's rationality, as non-rational dimensions are simpler and severe with rationality than many rational arguments, where each detail requires being addressed in detail to explain its real essence. Therefore, we will try to address ideas and concepts in a clear and precise manner so that these could be conveyed in a simpler and more profound way, using another kind of communication.

One of the main purposes of this work will be showing the need of surpassing the rational step entailing the analysis of reality and organizational and social relations in order to ascend towards the step of consciousness, where the human being recognizes him as an indivisible part integrated into a whole unified by essence.

The search for establishing a different approach begins by questioning the paradigms that determine and model modern institutions and organizations. An adequate questioning of effective paradigms allows considering the possibility that institutions and organizations evolve towards more advanced stages, offering the possibility of including in the field of organizational dimensions terms relating to the cooperation of persons, the overcoming of conflicts, consciousness, solidarity and harmony.

The possibility of offering an improved alternative to the way in which modern organizations and society itself are organized justifies the search for new paradigms to be be implemented. We deem necessary believing that it is possible indeed to envision reality in a different manner and also arranging institutions and organizations in another way. We have the conviction that evolution forms an intrinsic part of human beings and the institutions created by them, by invoking the hope that the world where we live can improve. This essay finds its most significant pillar in this last argument: considering that it is possible to give free rein to imagination and propose a fairer, more cooperative, more conscious and more harmonic social and organizational reality, through the establishment of an Organic Society.

This essay has 5 parts clearly differentiated, each with an established purpose, where each part finds its justification in integrating to the other parts: Human's behavior and Higher Principle, Organic Systems, the Organic Society, the Organic State and Processes of Change.

CHAPTER I

HUMAN'S BEHAVIOR AND HIGHER PRINCIPLE

For the implementation of an organic structure at organizational and social level, we deem important the analysis and synthesis of the psychological phenomena that form part of man's integration process to the social environment and the motives of its behavior in the course of such process. "To understand the dynamics of the social process we must understand the dynamics of the psychological processes operating within the individual, just as to understand the individual we must see him in the context of the culture which moulds him" (Fromm. 2016: 3). Therefore, it is of extreme importance studying some of the factors that have an incidencce in the behavior of individuals, especially those relating to motivation.

1. FACTORS THAT HAVE AN INFLUENCE ON BEHAVIOR

What motivates a person to act in a certain manner? What are the grounds for an individual's behavior? In order to address the behavior topic it is necessary to refer to the concept of motivation. Murray (1967) establishes that a motive is an internal factor that starts, drives and intgrates a person's behavior. Motivation differentiates itself from other factors that also have an influence on behavior, such as a person's experiences, his/her physical capabilities and the environment where the person is, although such factors also may have an influence on motivation. Murray divides motivation into two components: the internal drive that leads a person to act, and the reward, which finishes with motivation once the purpose is reached. Later, he adds the factor relating to the consciousness, as he establishes that motivation includes the conscious with to obtain something. The relationship between motivation and behavior is sometimes complex. Only after we know and learn something more about these complex effects of motivation, we will be ready to understand the human behavior (Murray. 1967).

1.1 Bare Necessities

For Maslow, necessities have a decissive influence on individuals' behavior motivation. The needs or necessities that are currently regarded as a starting point for the motivation theory are the so-called physiological impulses. There are a series of needs that are a priority in respect of human behavior (hunger, thirst, etc.). But, what happens to the wishes of a man when there is enough bread and when his stomach is regularly filled? Then, other higher-level needs emerge and these prevail above the body beyond the physiological level. And when these are satisfied, new ones appear (even higher than the previous ones) and so on. Basic human necessities are organized according to a hierarchy of relative predominance (Maslow. 1963). Thus, Maslow establishes the following hierarchy on the necessities that have an influence on man's behavior, in an increasing order: physiological necessities, safety necessities, affection necessities, self-esteem necessities, and self-fulfillment necessities.

The hierarchy established does not imply that a higher need or necessity will not appear until the lower one be satisfied in 100%, but that it may appear if it is mostly satisfied. For example: it is as if the average citizen was satisfied in 85% regarding his physiological necessities, 70% regarding his safety necessities, 50% his love necessities, 40% his self-appreciation necessities and 10%

his self-fulfillment necessities [...] Regarding the appearance of a new need after satisfying a predominant necessity, we may state that the latter does not emerge abruptly, but gradually instead, in small degrees, out of nowhere (Maslow. 1963).

The satisfaction of basic or bare necessities plays a fundamental role in individuals' behavior, but does not determine all the extents of behavior. Any behavior may become the channel that allows the flowing of several impulses. The overall essence of behavior is "multimotivated", where all basic necessities may exert their influence, more than just any of them specifically. Behavior is not esclusively motivated by basic necessities. Furthermore, not all of the entire behavior is motivated by them. There are many factors other than motives, such as the external environment. Behavior can be entirely determined by the external field, and even by external stimuli, specific and isolated.

1.2 The Need to be Related

Fromm (1952) establishes that physiological needs do not constitute the only aspect of the human nature with inevitable character. There is another part that is likewise compulsive, but not rooted to body processes, and which is part of the very essence of human life, in form and practice, as is "the need to be related to the world outside oneself, the need to avoid aloneness. To feel completely alone and isolated leads to mental disintegration just as physical starvation leads to death." (Fromm. 2016: 19).

Fromm states that such connection with other individuals has to do not only with physical contact, but with a relationship based on ideas, values, or at least social standards that grant the individual a sense of belonging. The lack of connection with values, symbols or standards, which may be called moral loneliness, is as intolerable as the physical loneliness. In other words, physical loneliness only becomes intolerable when is accompanied by moral loneliness. Thus, moral connection with the world may well adopt the shape of a solitary monk who believes in God or the political prisoner isolated from the rest of the persons, who feels, however, connected to his struggle mates. This need induces human beings to create connection forms with the external world, thus channeling the need to belong.

Later in this essay, the reader will be able to understand that the greatest connection there exists, the supreme connection, is the consciousness of being bonded to the rest of the Universe through Love. Knowing that one is part of the cosmic system which essence is Love, can enable any human being to resist the greatest challenges and trials, and to continue holding on to his path, with the conviction that this will lead him to the actual encounter, the encounter with himself, the true essence of the human being and the encounter with the rest of the existence. The sense of connection through Love does not allow anyone suffering in solitude, as even while being physicaly alone, the person knows that the rest of the Universe is in communion with him and conspires for him to go on. This kind of connection transcends both the physical and moral experience, and transforms itself into a wholesome experience, bringing to the material realm the consciousness of the spiritual plane.

1.3 Reason

The rational factor has a significant influence on the persons' behavior, especially in Western societies. Rationality has a strong presence in the motivation of modern man's behavior, making a large part of his reality to be inspired on and determined by reason.

Reason allows analyzing the diverse alternatives that a person may have before a problem, and in assessing the advantages and disadvantages *a priori*, this person makes a certain decision. There are a series of factors involved in this process relating to his experience, and to the "investment" to be made (efforts, resources, time, emotional load, etc.)

In general, reason serves as a tool to reach an objective based on a need. For example: 1) A mathematics problem or a science experiment require the almost exclusive use of reason to be solved, as the needs to be satisfied relate to self-esteem and personal fulfillment. 2) A war requires a large deal of planning and strategy, in addition to the political elements involved, factors which may be addressed in a rational manner. In this case, the needs would obey to a nature other than that implied in the first example, such as survival, safety, self-esteem or self-fulfillment.

But reason does not determine man's behavior per se, nor is it the sole factor that man resorts to make a decision, for there are a series of elements relating both to man's intrinsical nature (feelings, fears and/or wishes) and to his past experience, in addition to factors such as personality, achievement-driven motivation, good sense and global vision. There is the well-known case of persons who are experts in a specific area and who, before an unprecedented situation, require an adaptation time to make the right decision or even to go through an error-and-trial process, leading them to initially make "beginners' mistakes".

1.4 The Heart

Starting from the basis that man's behavior is not exclusively rational, it is worth determining what type of additional factors have an influence on man's motivation, always seeking to understand the ground for his behavior, and to ultimately design an organizational structure that meets people's needs and takes into consideration the diverse behavior factors of its participants. In this regard, emotional factors play a fundamental role in determining man's behavior. We will call such emotional factors *Heart*, that inner voice that represents both the emotional aspect and the inner wisdom, which leads the human being to try to integrate the surrounding world in a harmonious manner.

Hence, the example set by Gandhi helps us understand the Heart when he commenced with his first steps in South Africa, during the beginning of what was later known as "Satyagraha", closely linked to the non-violence "weapon" and the strength of the spirit, interpreted in the Eastern world as "Pacific Resistance", which Gandhi referred to as an incomplete interpretation of a philosophy based on the *Truth*[1] (Gandhi. 1958).

---

[1]   To Gandhi, the definition of Truth constituted a difficult matter to solve, and however, he resolved it by establishing that it was the *inner voice* that each person has. Truth lies in each human Heart and each person must seek it there and allow oneself to be guided accordingly. But at the same time, he establishes that no one has the right to force anyone to make anything according to his conception of the Truth. Fromm also establishes the existence of a natural inner voice relating the values of justice and truth. "We have also reason to assume that (...) the striving for justice and truth is an inherent trend of human nature" (Fromm. 2016: 242).

Gandhi went to work to South Africa at the beginning of the XX century, with the purpose of working as a lawyer, but circumstances made him lead the movement for the defense of the rights of the Hindu community, before a regime that was oppressing them and took advantage of their needs. Thus, he became the community's spokesman and representative to demand the respect of their civil rights, acting as mediator before the South African government. During such process moments of violence and exarcebation rose, making many times the efforts that were being made to lose their constructive purpose. Mahatma had to call upon the Heart to calm the circumstances down and be able to continue in the right direction. In this regard he states:

> "Up to the year 1906, I simply relied on appeal to reason (…) But I found that reason failed to produce an impression when the critical moment arrived in South Africa (…) if you want something really important to be done you must not merely satisfy the reason, you must move the heart also" (Gandhi. 2016: 109-110).

Thus, Gandhi's rational approach led to a way of being where it was also important to address people's heart, in order to gain their trust and not to miss a pacifist way of doing things. This change of attitude was worth pursuing, as the whole reivindication process for defending Hindi's community rights provided good results with no violence.

Satyagraha was subsequently implemented in India, which led to the Independence from the British Empire. Once more, appeal to people's heart showed a valid, necessary and efficient way to reach the ultimate goal. Among various activities implemented, it is worth mentioning Gandhi's long fasts so that reason and Heart found a common way to erradicate violence and overcome divergences.

Accepting the Heart as an important driver for human behavior enables the emergence of a different perspective for human reality, where mutual understanding, accepting others aspirations, and wishing for living in harmony, allows to set up a multiple dialogue where all people's necessities are recognized and potentially met. The Heart sets conditions for transforming wishes and dreams to projects and accomplishments through hope and social harmony, which by the way, are not easy to describe through rational means.

1.5 Consciousness

Historically, the concept of consciousness has had two different approaches (Gomes Penna. 1985): a) consciousness is a biological phenomenon of a highly developed nervous system; b) consciousness reflects human being's social condition; more specifically, man's necessity to communicate with human beings (sociological approach).

The sociological perspective sets various levels of consciousness regarding man's relationship to others. There are selfish people, only caring about their needs; others whom are aware of their needs, but also about others; and then the alutristic ones, only caring about the needs of others. All these terms are defined from a relative and subjective standpoint. There are people only looking to obtain benefits from the system, and there are those that aside from gaining benefits, they also want to give back to the system, willing and looking to provide a service to the same system that keeps them alive. What is the difference between these two types of people?

Consciousness is the answer. A person may appraise what is best for himself as an individual, for him and his team, for the organization/company, for society, or even, what is best for the planet, depending on his level of consciousness. The higher the level of consciousness, the more likely someone is to care about his social and environmental surroundings and the more the wellbeing of others impacts his own. Consciousness enables you to connect your life experiences with those of others. The higher the level of consciousness, the more feasible it will be to find balance between individual and collective wellbeing.

The level of consciousness is not measurable, but it may be inferred from people's accomplishments. They speak on behalf of a person; they are his business cards, the outcome of who someone truly is. Someone's heart may be appraised thanks to the Love he puts on his duties, even though Love itself cannot be seen. Likewise, consciousness may not be measured clearly and precisely, but it can be seen through someone's actions.

When someone increases his level of consciousness, he becomes more aware of the wellbeing of others. Fromm (1952) states that relating to others is fundamental to people's mental and emotional health. Each individual is born, grows, and develops surrounded by people, in a city or the countryside. Other people make part of his life. It is not likely to choose to eliminate contact with other human. Not even a hermit who voluntarily chooses to live in isolation has eliminated contact with people, because recollections of his past contact with others make up part of his day-to-day world.

Based on this, we must say that other people make up part of someone's life even when one is not aware of this. Thus, *other people are an integral part of someone's world, even that he may not be mindful of that.* Hence, it is not possible to consider someone's life totally isolated from the rest of the world. His life, activities, job, and day-to-day events are strictly related and concatenated to other people.

As a result, we may state that the rest of the social environment makes part of an individual. An important portion of someone's life is composed by the individuals surrounding him; meaning that, *all individuals are integral part of a person's realm.* A person's behavior and his daily activities are determined by his societal sorroundings, conventions, ethics codes, family relationships (existing or non-existing), or even by a rebellious behavior against the establishment.

The rest of the social world does not exist as an external agent to the individual, but as an integral part of him. This statement allows us to overcome the fragmental approach of social relationships, where individuals are considered isolated beings, and be substituted with an integral vision, where every individual is unique, but sees the rest of the social world as part of him.

This approach makes us understand that an individual's well-being depends on his well-being plus that of others. It would be difficult for someone to consider himself as being well if those around him are in need, even if personal needs are satisfied. If someone is well fed, he will not feel completely satisfied if he perceives that those around him are starving.

This same approach may be applied to the case when someone kills another on purpose. When someone kills for the first time, something dies inside of him as well. This may be respect for the life of others, social inclusion, willingness to help others, or compassion for his fellowmen. When someone kills another, it in turn kills something inside of him as well, that may keep him from being part of the world he was part of until that moment. When someone kills, stop being the person he was, and becomes someone else. Thus, *when someone kills, he himself dies as well.*

Under the same perspective but from a positive standpoint, we may review what happens when someone helps another. In this case, this individual is helping not only someone else, but himself as well. When someone helps another, a nice feeling surges, making sense to his life, and being fulfilled of making another's life better. When someone helps another, this individual overcomes his individuality and separateness, to become part of something bigger: humankind, allowing himself to be part of other's world, and proving that two different worlds may become one for a moment. Hence, *when someone helps another, he helps himself as well.*

Something different happens when someone charges others for his service. We are not sure exactly why, but the feeling of giving something to someone and subsequently charging is different. The service provider is not being fulfilled by the same feeling as if he was not charging. He gave something for something in return. His ultimate goal was to receive, to help himself. From this standpoint, helping others unselfishly is more harmonious than looking for something in return. But, being open for receiving is important as well. This behavior causes the surge of integration to the social environment.

It is worth mentioning that helping oneself is important as well. Harmony consists of considering oneself as part of the others as well. Thus, it is equally important working towards our own well-being. A harmonious relationship with the social environment sets our well-being and that of others in the same level, in a global dynamic where the ultimate goal is the well-being of all. Hence, *a balanced-harmonious-integrated social environment is fundamentally composed by individuals where one-self and others well-being are equally important.*

Accepting that others make up part of ourselves sets the conditions to understand that giving and receiving are equally important, and that *we all make up part of a unified whole.* This will allow the surge of a social order based more on harmonious principles than conflictive ones.

A plant provides a good organic example of a harmonious behavior among its components: every cell has a role to keep the plant alive, where each one's mission is equally important as other's, within a dynamic nature where the plant living is their priority. Every cell tries to obtain no more from the organic environment than the others (i.e. food, oxygen, etc.) to accomplish their mission, each and every one working to keep an overall balance.

Under the same perspective, a social structure may be established where balance and harmony between all components (i.e. people) are the leading principles, and may rise a system where every person's well-being is equally important.

Being aware that every other being is part of ourselves and that every human's well-being is as important as others, will let us create a system where the illusion of *separateness* can be superseded by *integration* with regards to personal, social and organizational relationships. This is about consciousness. Men/women make up part of themselves, their entourage, and the rest of the Universe. People are not separate beings from the social structure, but an intrinsic being of it, where they live, grow, develop, and die.

Hence, the analysis where parts are separated, reviewed, and put together again is incomplete. Only an integral analysis of human being, where his social and natural surroundings are included may give rise to a harmonious and cooperative social order.

1.6 Other factors

The following factors should be considered for an integral analysis of human behavior, but it is out of the scope of this essay to assess them in detail: intuition, unconscious, and the external field.

Intuition is a perception channel of reality not perceived by the natural 5 senses; it describes the ability to understand without the use of reason. Through intuition, an individual senses events and situations, sometimes even without being aware of it. In general, consciousness is not part of this type of perception. When someone follows his intuition, he might modify his conduct or make another choice without being aware of the real sources of motivation. Intuition is real, and modifies people's behavior under certain circumstances.

When someone follows his intuition, he tends to act in a way not easily understood by others. Moreover, this individual himself may not be aware of the source of his behavior, but he is certain that he is doing the right thing. Modern man has stopped modifying his behavior to follow his intuition, due to the predominance of senses perception and use of reason. But intuition is real, even though it has not been supported and/or demonstrated.

In our modern world, everything is explained through cause and effect relationships. But when someone wants to predict the future based on cause and effect, he will rarely nail it. Reality is hard to predict due to many factors not considered or included in our forecast models. Reality is a complex web of causes and effects, many of them not easily discernible. One of the greatest challenges for modern man, is trying to make the right choice by finding the right balance between senses, reason and intuition.

Sometimes, an individual acts in a certain way and makes a choice with for no apparent reason when facing a situation. This corresponds to an intuitive behavior, based on past experiences or a non-rational perception of reality - to a non-conscious reflex that makes the right choice at the right time. Intuition may be considered a sixth sense, in addition to the natural five ones.

The **Unconscious** is an important factor in human behavior. The unconscious comprises all elements repressed by education (Freudian psychology), and the so-called collective unconscious (Jung, 1955). "It must be pointed out that just as the human body shows a common anatomy over and above all racial differences, so, too, the psyche possesses a common substratum transcending all differences in culture and consciousness. I have called this substratum the collective unconscious. This unconscious psyche, common to all mankind, does not consist merely of contents capable of becoming conscious, but of latent dispositions towards certain identical reactions" (Jung, 2016). The unconscious affects human behavior, in addition to the above factors.

Maslow talks about the **external field** as an important factor for human behavior. The external field exerts its influence either on the consciousness or unconscious. It may come as cultural influence, traditions, social conventions, moral, fashion, copied customs, etc.

1.7 Relationship between all factors

The relationship between all factors above will be considered, as well as how an ethical intent for human behavior modification should address a call to people's conscience.

Bare necessities have a great influence in human behavior. They make up part of a process where an individual becomes aware of a necessity, and then makes a choice for satisfying it. Examples: 1) A man is hungry, he wants to eat, he evaluates different options for satisfying his hunger, and chooses the most convenient one, either by proximity (i.e. going to his fridge), or by price (choose between going to a fast food or a restaurant), or going hunting. Thus, he made his choice after perceiving his hunger, and evaluating his options. 2) When someone is facing a threatening wild animal, he wants to be safe again. He assesses the situation and evaluates his options, be it escaping or attacking back, and then makes a choice for surviving. So, he became aware of danger and evaluated his options quickly before making a choice. Both situations show how the behavior was preceded by the necessity awareness. In general, necessity awareness precedes the action or behavior.

Reason and **Heart** go through a conscious path before modifying human behavior. An individual tends to evaluate different options based on his Heart and Reason, trying to balance what he thinks with what he feels. This will not grant a balance between both factors. Generally speaking, one prevails over the other, depending on the person's profile. The more conscious someone is, the more the Heart will prevail. When someone's consciousness increases, the Heart tends to prevail over Reason.

A person's behavior may be modified by his **Intuition** without being necessarily conscious about it. The **unconsciousness** affects/modifies behavior without the individual being aware of the sources of motivation. The **external field** exerts influence on various factors, including reason, heart, consciousness, and unconsciousness.

In summary, bare necessities affect human behavior, as well as consciousness, which are influenced by reason and heart. These three factors are inter-related, and have greatest influence on behavior, but they are affected as well by intuition, unconsciousness, and the external field.

The consciousness – heart – reason relationship is represented below:

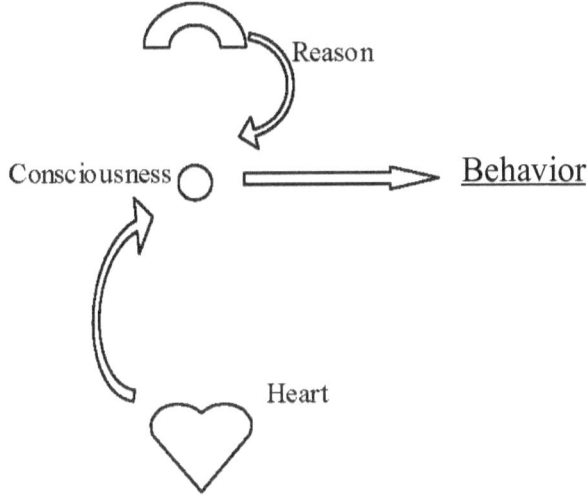

Fig. 1.1: Main factors influencing human behavior

Human behavior is not influenced accurately by any of the factors above, like a cause-effect relationship resulting in a certain behavior through a specific input of them. Human behavior cannot be predicted in advance, given the complexity of human being sources of motivation. But, certain predictive behaviour can be established based on an individual level of consciousness. The higher the level of consciousness, the more an individual will integrate himself harmoniously to his social environment, by listening to his heart.

In any case, the goal here is not to determine human behavior in advance to achieve certain results, but to understand which factors affect human behavior, so that a harmonious human social system may be created. Above all, these understandings and subsequent hypothetical actions should be subject to *free will*, where every human being has the possibility and the right to live at liberty, based on his wishes, aspirations, and respect to others rights, wishes, and aspirations. A person should live in accord with the *Principle of Freedom*:

> "Human existence begins when the lack of fixation of action by instincts exceeds a certain point; when the adaptation to nature loses its coercive character; when the way to act is no longer fixed by hereditarily given mechanisms. In other words, human existence and freedom are from the beginning inseparable" (Fromm, 1942).

Based on the Principle of Freedom, we deem it necessary to design a social system where people are free to behave harmoniously, without being forced to be individualistic and selfish due to prevailing current socio-economical conventions, but to behave collaboratively and with solidarity, as long as their level of consciousness guides them to do so.

2. MODIFICATION OF HUMANS'S BEHAVIOR

What makes humans change their behavior? If we start from the principle that all factors above influence human behavior, some individuals will pay attention to some factors more than others depending on their level of consciousness. A "low" level of consciousness will make some factors have greater influence on someone's behavior (i.e. bare necessities, or the external field). But, the greater the level of consciousness, the more balance there will be among all factors and the greater the role of the Heart.

Where does a social change start? Which factor unleashes a modification in human behavior? All factors above may unleash a behavior modification, either individually or in a group. Actually, a certain change may be "multimotivated", driven by a combination of factors. In order to establish a more harmonious social system, it may be decided at a higher level (i.e. government) to influence a given internal or external factor. But, ethical considerations lead us to affirm that *any human behavior modification set to establish a harmonious social system should be driven by an increase in the level of consciousness.*

Every ethical social change should start with a raise of individuals' awareness - of them, their surroundings, social environment, and the planet - allowing them to increase their level of consciousness while exercising their autonomy, and being integrated to their social environment. A change in human behavior via an increased level of consciousness, addresses the internal processes that results in permanent changes, due to the resulting connection with the real human essence, and respecting the Principle of Freedom and the rights of others at the same time.

When bare necessities are satisfied, an individual's level of consciousness tend to increase, because this individual is free to fulfill a superior level of necessities, after having fulfilled the lower level ones (i.e. the desire to learn after hunger is satisfied). But, consciousness can determine the type of necessities as well. Maslow (1963) addresses the case of people that have fulfilled their necessities over their entire life, especially during their first years of life. They usually develop an exceptional ability to bear frustration over their entire life, thanks to a healthy and strong structure of character. They are the ones who withstand any disagreement or opposition, go against the current of public opinion, and defend their truth against all odds, including their personal integrity. *They are those who have loved and been loved, who can stand firm against social rejection and prosecution.*

In order to increase the level of social harmony, it may be sound to satisfy all individuals' **bare necessities**. However, there is no guarantee that this process will be successful, because some individual's selfishness may transform this process into a fight for getting their necessities more satisfied than those of others, reducing harmony and increasing inequality.

We may also try to convince all individuals to live in harmony by **rational** means. But, the outcome of this approach has not proven succesful to reach this goal in Modern Societies, through modern paradigms (individualism, rationality, market economy, and efficiency). Modern democratic societies show bigger inequality between the richest and the poorest more and more. On the other side, History shows how totalitarian regimes have proven wrong to reach equality through oppression. Rationality has not been enough to fulfill the requirements of convincing everyone for a better collective order for all.

We may try to modify the **external field**, setting up a system with the right techniques of stimulus and response, aiming to modify behavior to a more collaborative approach. This was already proposed by Skinner (1977) with his Behaviorism. But this is ethically questionable. It establishes that man's behavior is basically and mostly controlled by external forces, ignoring internal factors such as Heart, reason, intuition, and consciousness. Besides, the ultimate intent should not be creating human robots controlled by certain inputs and getting the right outputs, but to *design social and organizational systems that satisfy the right of living in a more harmonious way, in a free will environment.*

We may try to act upon human **consciousness**, showing the necessity of living together peacefully for an overall well-being, based on accepting Love as the strongest force in the Universe, through an educational process that teaches man that he makes up part of a universal reality essentially harmonious; that makes him see the advantages of collaboration and solidarity, based on a balance between our own well-being and that of others; and that makes us all have a global thinking, where all components depend on one another. *We firmly believe this is the best approach to reach a mutual understanding, and to design a social reality respectful of human dignity and the planet that is our dwelling.*

Therefore, by combining the **principle of freedom** and human behavior modification via **an increase in consciousness**, we may create a social system driven by humanistic values to provide people the freedom to live in a more harmonious way. By accepting that human behavior may be led by our level of consciousness guided by the Heart, more than the other factors involved, we may dream of a reality where the **Law of Love** becomes true, and solidarity and collaboration become fundamental pillars of these social and organizational structures.

2.1 Increase in the Consciousness Level

The creation of a more harmonious social reality will only become true if human behavior modification towards more collaborative levels is achieved via an increase in people's consciousness. Any other way to achieve this goal may be seen as a manipulation of human beings. Therefore, the ultimate goal should be to increase their level of consciousness. But, how can this be achieved?

This may be accomplished by satisfying people's bare necessities and looking to simultaneously raise awareness, basing this last one on an educational process, by teaching people the advantages of living under the *organic paradigm* to achieve a general well-being, and seeing life as a global, interactive, interrelated, and integrated reality.

Just like it happened with *rationality*, which became a paradigm thanks to the results obtained from the scientific method application, that defined and founded the pilots of our modern society; the same may happen with the *organic paradigm*, through an educational process that calls for an increase in human consciousness to a higher level, showing the benefits of peaceful coexistence amongst men, designing the foundations of organic organizations and institutions, defining a harmonious relationship with our natural environment, and accepting that everyone makes up an essential part of this wonderful cosmic reality.

We are convinced that all human beings were born to socialize with others harmoniously; that a world can be created where physical violence and wars disappear forever; that all disagreements between people, communities, and countries can be solved through a continuous dialogue and mutually enriching understanding; that people can relate to others based on a constant trade of help and benefits, understanding that we all make up part of the same race, have the same fate, and are part of the same world. Humans are able to build what they can imagine. Then, has the time come to imagine the advent of an era of peace – collaboration – solidarity – harmony? The answer to this question may be affirmative. Could this be just imagination or time for it to come true?

3. PARTIAL CONCLUSIONS

According to the above, the following partial conclusions may be established:

1) Humans cannot be represented only as rational beings in order to deal properly with motivational factors in organizational and social systems.
2) Factors other than reason should be included in the sources of motivation of people, like Heart, consciousness and intuition.
3) The higher the level of consciousness, the more the Heart will influence someone's behavior, and the more balance there will be between all motivational factors.
4) Main human motivational factors (Heart, reason, consciousness and intuition) should be taken into consideration to properly design and model organizational and social systems.
5) The rational paradigm should be replaced with the organic paradigm for modeling and designing organic social systems.

4. ORGANIZATION'S PRINCIPLES

Science requires evidence of observed facts even when that in some cases no demonstration is required (i.e. gravity); so, when facing a new concept or paradigm, this new concept should either be demonstrated, or it may be put into practice to see if it works.

Science requires proof to increase our understanding; but reality goes on independently of this proof. When we accept a new concept or paradigm, reality does not necessarily change, but our understanding of it does; as it happened with Einstein's Theory of Relativity: reality did not change, but our understanding of our reality did.

The same applies when trying to set up a harmonious social and organizational paradigm; we either try to demonstrate that it works before putting it into practice or, we assume it may be true, and try to design a social order that follows organic principles, then we can evaluate if it works. It is worth going ahead with this second option, just for the fact of applying organic principles to our social systems and organizations.

a. Organicity

We live in a wonderful harmonious natural world. When analyzing plants, ecosystems, sub-atomic world, the cosmos, or the human body, we can appreciate how complex natural systems are. However, if we look further and to try to identify their essence, we may see a common **unicity** based on harmonious natural processes.

Rather than talking about complexity or **unicity**, we might talk about *Organicity*: a wider, deeper and simpler concept that indicates how an organic system works. This concept is not only about biological systems, but also about natural systems with similar characteristics. It covers practically every system existing in the Universe: atoms, molecules, biological beings, ecosystems, star systems, galaxies, etc. The main characteristic of organic systems is that they behave like living beings, where internal processes are handled harmoniously and with flexibility to ensure their survival, never trying to obtain more than required from their environment, discarding what they do not need, and having a series of properties common in biological systems: birth, growth, reproduction, adaptation, differentiation, flexibility, integration and evolution. When we talk about organicity, we talk as well about an intrinsically concept belonging to every natural system: *harmony*.

When approaching organizational and social structures under the *organic paradigm*, we will see them as living beings, with similar characteristics and structure. To this end, organic systems harmony should be highlighted.

Other than social systems created by men, we see a natural reality intrinsically harmonious, where all evolutionary processes flow smoothly. A plant growing, a living being's conception, the ecosystem's balance, a human body functioning, the climatic balance, and traslation of stars make up part of an organic reality widely accepted by humans, without having been demonstrated.

Harmony is revealed by the fact that all components of each of the structures mentioned above has a specific function and is integrated properly to their system, without occupying another component's space or fulfilling another component's role. In the case of a plant, each one of the cells has a role and is integrated to the whole system, allowing the plant to live and grow harmoniously.

Man can witness how he is inserted into a cosmic and universal reality harmoniously. Planets rotate around the Sun; the Moon rotates around the Earth, all of them supporting our planet weather balance, based on an intrinsically harmonious balance allowing the existence of living beings. Plants, animal life, rain, seasons, seabeds and the food chain happen in a balance where harmony and integration make up a fundamental part of Earth's ecosystems. Nothing is steady, everything flows. All living systems preserve their essence, and they are integrated to all other systems.

The human body is fundamentally harmonious. Internal processes flow as a perfect synchronized dance where every organ is integrated with the others, allowing human beings to live. Physics shows the harmonious movement of natural objects, from planets to atoms, embedded in a universal balance that makes them be born, grow, develop, and die, in a continuous recycling process of matter and energy. Socially speaking, men and superior animals show a natural tendency of living in communities, a behavior to gather together in herds, taking advantage of solidarity and social organization. Men show a strong tendency towards social behavior, collaboration is the dominant feature, and from a biological standpoint, the most important one (Darin-Drabkin, 1962).

Based on the above, we start from the premise that nature (and man is part of this) is fundamentally harmonious. One of the biggest conflicts of human beings is knowing that they belong intrinsically to this wonderful order, but they are forced to think separately. This happened when the man entered the Modern world (Marcuse, 1973), leaving behind his integration to the natural order, and splitting from his natural surroundings and human peers, to see himself as a separate being, and as a mechanical structure made up of multiple elements acting together. Then, he forgot that for many years he saw the universal reality like a grand concert directed by a divine Hand.

In this regard, we share the integrated vision of man with nature by Fromm:

"The emergence of man from nature is a long-drawn-out process; to a large extent he remains tied to the world from which he emerged; he remains part of nature – the soil he lives on, the sun and moon and stars, the trees and flowers, the animals, and the group of people with whom he is connected by the ties of blood. Primitive religions bear testimony to man's feeling of oneness with nature. Animate and inanimate nature are part of his human world or, as one may also put it, he is still part of the natural world." (Fromm. 2016: 32 -33)

Therefore, our efforts should be now to create social and organizational systems inspired by the *organic paradigm*, calling for man's consciousness for social integration, and aligned with the natural reality he is part of.

By accepting social and organizational harmony, we are not denying the need for diversity or open discussion about any matter, or reducing free will for setting up a reality where people's material aspirations are met. Our proposal is based on designing a social reality where the conditions are set for individuals to be part of a harmonious social and natural system, to boost their individual evolution and the society's that they make part of in a more fluid way.

Why man designs social and organizational systems based on conflicts (i.e. competition)? One answer may be due to the way he sees life: in a fragmented way. When rationality is too present in man's life, he starts missing the big picture and harmony of every natural process, making him focus further on these processes, forgetting that the starting point of viewing things microscopically was to understand the reality as a whole. From a rational standpoint, it is not easy to relate to others harmoniously, because society is not seen as an organic being, but as a group of separate people acting together, each one of them following his own path. However, there is a way to overcome this point of view: to base human relationships not on reason, but on the awareness that *we all make up part of a unified whole*. Nature is like that. Man is no different. He makes up part of nature, and therefore, he should be able to design a social reality based on his essence.

Our proposal will design a social and organizational reality to deal properly with all indicated behavioral factors, to work together and collaborate, setting up the conditions for an increasing behaviural momentum of collaboration and solidarity. Thus, we will design a structure based on conscious and *organic* principles, rather than rational and mechanistic ones.

b. Principle of the Harmonic Organization

The rational paradigm has shaped human relationships in modern organizations based on individual contribution, functionality, and the service employees will provide to achieve the ultimate goal: profit. From the employee's point of view, this relationship is shaped by what he receives from the firm, with regards to income, benefits, and career status. In this relationship, every part tries to get the most at the lowest possible cost: the firm will try to pay less, and employees to earn more.

This tends to cause conflicts in the employment relationship, due to the fact that the company's goals differ from the employees'. This is the reason why organizational theories have existed for many years, trying to alleviate this conflict, which consists of an increasing discomfort in existing organizations, that turns into individual unhappiness and organizational inefficiency (Leite, 1995). This conflict exists both in private companies and public sector, making this a widely spread issue.

How may their goals (employees' and organizations') merge into one? So far, no organizational theory has stated that an organization's and employees' goals should be one. Actually, they are considered inversely proportional: the higher the employee's income, the less profit for the company, and vice versa. For an employee to increase his income, one of the following conditions should be met: either by an increase of employees' productivity, thus reducing costs and having more income allocated to the payroll; or by distributing part of the company's existing profit among employees. As we can see, they are conflicting interests.

Every company has an identity, defined by a series of parameters that identify its uniqueness, bringing along terms used to describe a person: company interest, income, values, etc. Some of these terms' goals differ from the employees', who, if facing the choice between their own interests and the company's, will tend to choose theirs.

Merger attempts between organization's and employees' goals have not met expectations, basically because they are conflictive. When trying to join both entities' goals, the final result is not satisfying for any of them, being in the mid-point between both final interests, and leaving both parties unsatisfied.

Besides, both parties' merger attempts question modern organization paradigms, based on profit and resources management; and suggest the emergence of different paradigms, where the employees' aspirations and goals are as important as the firm's. Thus, the final result of modern organizational theories is a fuzzy combination of means and ends.

Both parties' goals merging involve means and ends meeting as well, because it will translate organizational reality into one. This will imply the emergence of a different organization, based on other paradigms. Therefore, *both the company's and employees' goals merging entail the modern organization disappearance and the emergence of another kind of organization.*

This other type of organization should be based on different principles. Hereafter, an important principle will be considered to combine both parties' goals into one, and among other things, eradicate conflict within organizations.

c. Higher Principle: the Law of Love

A different type of organization should be based on a different paradigm in order to replace modern organizations. The search for this new paradigm may be provided by natural systems.

Insects' social organizations are well known for their order and organization based on instincts. But "instinct (…) is a diminishing if not a disappearing category in higher animal forms, especially in the human" (Fromm, 2016). Hence, we should start looking for a principle that provides the organizational role in lower animals in the scale of development, but present in human systems. A general principle should be found to guide human consciousness, and influence behavior towards a more harmonious pattern. Additionally, this principle should satisfy both Heart and Reason.

After several attempts to find such principle, we believe that the right one to guide human behavior and model human organizations towards more harmonious expressions, is the greatest emotion a human may feel, the most subtle and wonderful force existing in the Universe, the energy that leads humans to accomplish great deeds, that which makes someone gives his life to save other, the Muse for poets and acclaimed authors, the motive that expresses the most subtle rationale and the source of inspiration for the greatest works of humankind: **Love**.

Love is a principle and a metaphor, it can be seen as a way of traveling or as an end goal; as a universal emotion or as a superior ideal for humankind; as a star on the horizon showing the path to follow, or as the waves and wind that shape the sea.

Love may be seen as a principle for organizations, as an option, as a call for consciousness, or as life itself. Love allows someone to consider others part of him. When someone loves, he gives without expecting anything in return; but he is willing to receive, as part of a dynamic of mutual understanding and surrender. When someone loves another, he takes care of him, makes him part of himself, and is willing to reduce his well-being to support that of his. We are not talking only about romantic love, *but about the emotion that makes people consider others as part of themselves. Love* drives harmonious choices in the right direction, and makes people see the well-being of others as part of theirs.

Had *Love* been proven by scientists as a fundamental principle for life and intrinsical source of order for the Universe, our conception of reality would change dramatically. But why do we have to wait for this discovery if it can provide support for creating a harmonious social reality as a hypothesis? The only possible answer is not having a level of consciousness high enough to imagine a harmonious, collaborative, and supportive social reality.

By accepting the *Law of Love,* along with a general increase in people's level of consciousness to the *organic level,* man should be able to dream and work for the establishment of more harmonious organizational and social systems, without the need of using rational means of control.

Based on the conviction that we all make up part of an intrinsically harmonious natural reality, and the feasibility of designing a social reality guided by the *Law of Love*, we will run the risk of proposing a social reality based on collaborative and human principles, where human kindness will be allowed to make up part of the design of the system.

Relevant aspects of the organic structure and its application on social and organizational systems will be addressed in the next chapter.

CHAPTER 2

ORGANIC SYSTEMS

"The Universe should be seen as a living being
rather than a big machine"

1. CONVENIENT PERSPECTIVE

A major debate occurred during the XIX century in the mathematical world which will support our proposal for the use of a different paradigm for reviewing modern organizations, to replace the mechanicist-bureaucratic one currently in place.

1.1 The Geometry of Euclid, Lobatchevsky and Riemann

Poincaré[2] (1984), a French mathematician, established that geometry is based on a certain number of non-demonstrable axioms (conventions). For a long time, many mathematicians tried to demonstrate Euclid's fifth postulate in vain (one of the basics of geometric calculus), which states that given any straight line and a point not on it, there "exists one and only one straight line which passes" through that point and never intersects the first line, no matter how far they are extended (fig. 2.1).

---

[2]   Jules-Henri Poincaré (1854-1912), Physics and Celestial Mechanics at University of Paris in the XIX century. He was described as *The Last Universalist* by his contemporaries, since he excelled in all fields of the discipline as it existed during his lifetime. He was member of all scientific societies of his time.

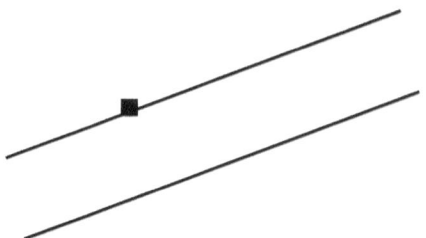

Fig. 2.1: Two parallel lines and point on one line

During the first quarter of the XIX century, Lobatchevsky (Russian) and Riemann (German) irrefutably demonstrated that this was impossible. Lobatchevsky inverted the problem in his intent to demonstrate the postulate. He established that given any straight line and a point not on it, there exists more than one line that passes through that point and never intersects the first line. Then, he deduced a series of theorems with no contradiction whatsoever between them (Poincaré. 1984). He ended up building a geometry as consistent as Euclid's, but incompatible with it. From that moment on, mathematics was questioned in its absolute validity. There were now two different ways of approaching mathematics.

Almost simultaneously, Riemann built up a geometry as flawless as Euclid's, but removing not only the 5th postulate, but the 1st as well, according to which only one straight line segment can be drawn joining any two points. The issue was that it was not consistent with Euclid's or Lobatchevsky's geometries. Incidentally, Riemann's geometry is the closest to Einstein's Theory of Relativity.

If these three geometries are valid although they are not consistent with each other, one might ask: which geometry is true?

Poincaré tackled this issue. Every geometry was based upon certain number of axioms, which were accepted as true. Poincaré concluded that geometrical axioms were not irrefutable truths, but rather conventions. Then, he asked himself which geometry was true: Euclid's, Lobatchevsky's or Riemann's? He came to the conclusion that this question did not make sense, *because one geometry is not more true than the other, but more convenient.* A geometry is not true, but rather convenient depending on each specific case.

Euclid's geometry is more convenient for our tridimensional and Newtonian world, to tackle and solve geometrical problems. But in the Relativity world, Euclid's geometry is limited and unable to face Einstenian realities, whereas Riemann's geometry is more suitable to do so.

1.2 The Convenient Perspective at organizational level

Following this line of thinking, we can establish a series of similar remarks to organizational and social systems, between mechanicist and organic approaches. The mechanicist-bureaucratic perspective sets the following organizational and social paradigms/conventions:

a) Human being behavior is guided mainly by reason; and
b) Organizations and social systems are composed by parts that can be reviewed separately and put back together for better understanding and functionality.

Based on the assumption that this approach can be contested, a different organizational model may be created based on the organic paradigm, in order to build an alternative organizational structure, which will be called henceforth the "organic structure".

Both the mechanicist-bureaucratic and the organic approaches are founded on paradigms and conventions that are not necessarily true, but support the creation of their correspondent structures.

The organic approach sees the organization as a living being - meaning it sees it as a net-structure where the unit and the structure make an indivisible whole, both being equally important. People are considered more than simply resources: they are the major players and beneficiaries of the organization.

2. ORGANIC PARADIGM

In the organizational modeling field, the term "organic" usually applies to a set of organizational techniques designed to increase the flexibility of traditional structures, by means of improving decision-making, increasing the use of information technology, encouraging horizontal relationships, and decentralizing structures. This term was made to differentiate more flexible structures from the rigid mechanicist-bureaucratic ones.

In the present case, the term "organic" will be used to denote *an organizational net-structure which can be modeled as an organic system, with properties specific to organic beings, such as adaptation, integration, collaboration, equilibrium and flexibility.*

The organic structure is a very powerful tool for modeling social, organizational and natural structures. Just like organizations may be represented as mechanical systems, including parts and processes by means of the organizational mechanicist-bureaucratic modeling tool; organizations may be represented as organic structures, establishing similarities with living beings and systems by means of the organic structure tool. From the atom to the Universe, going through biological beings, all systems may be modeled as organic structures.

The organic structure tool will be detailed as follows; it will include a description of conventions, properties, and characteristics that can be applied to organizational and social systems according to the organic paradigm.

2.1 Organic structure conventions

Two conventions are deemed necessary to discuss the organic structure characteristics and properties:

Reality can be represented as an organic structure: natural, organizational and social realities can be represented as organic structures, as well as the units and sub-structures that make up part of them. That is, they can be modeled as net-structures with organic systems characteristics.

People's behaviors are based on their level of consciousness: people's behaviors are determined by their level of consciousness. Social and organizational organic structures can work properly only if the people that make up part of it behave according to the organic level of consciousness, which is defined as *the level of consciousness where someone considers others' well-being as important as his own.* This level of consciousness will drive a harmonious, fair and integrated social structure.

2.2 Organic Structure

The net-structure is of fundamental importance in the organic approach. Every unit is related to other units via a network made up of similar units equally important. As part of this approach, every *unit has the autopoiesis property*[3], which means that every unit is a self-contained system of individual characteristics, related to other similar units. As a whole, they form a bigger reference system, with particular characteristics from the units, plus additional characteristics resulting from being a system. This bigger system may be considered as a unit making up part of a much bigger system, and so on.

From an organizational standpoint, a person may be considered a unit related to other similar units, such as his colleagues. As a whole, they are considered a working unit. This working unit may be considered a unit related to other working units with similar characteristics; but as a whole, they can be seen as a department, related to other departments, and so on. From the micro to the macro, the following may be considered as units and/or systems: person, working team, department, area, organization, market, multiple markets, international markets, and the global market.

---

[3]   The term "autopoiesis" was introduced by Maturana and Varela (1980). The term refers to the property of biological systems of being integrated by units that may be considered systems as well. For example: the human body is a unit composed by organs (units), which are composed by units themselves (i.e. tissues, cells, etc.).

The *Autopoiesis Principle of the Unit* is important for shaping the organic structure concept. In this regard, the unit identifies the space where it exists by its properties and the interaction with other units (Maturana and Varela. 1980). Every structure may be considered either a unit or a system, and this is dependent on how the structure is seen. A person may be seen as a unit and his working unit as the system. On a higher level, the working unit may be seen as a unit, and the department as the system, and so forth.

The **Organic Paradigm** is based on the Autopoiesis principle. As such, the organic system has the property of having the same type of structure anywhere in the system: the organic structure. Reality is being viewed as a big organic structure where the same type of structure is replicated everywhere in the system. Any given organic system is made up of an organic structure with multiple units, systems, and connections, where this same type of structure can be found when zooming in or zooming out from every existing unit (fig. 2.2).

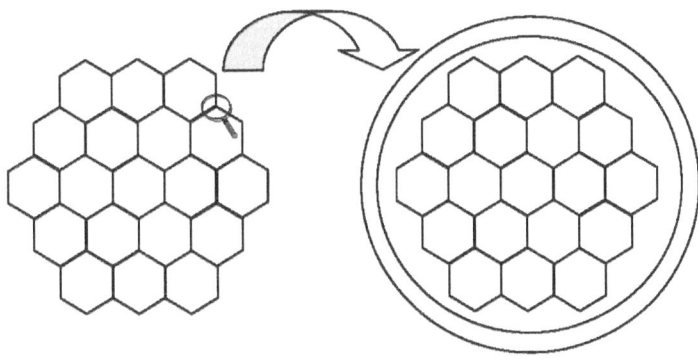

Fig. 2.2 – Organic structure

2.3 Properties of the Organic Structure

Adaptation: The organic organizational structure has the capability to adapt to local conditions in order to survive.

Autonomy: Every unit has the characteristic of fulfilling its function under the most convenient manner, as long as it is properly integrated to the rest of the system.

Autopoiesis: This property refers to the functionality of the living systems, where all units are autonomous, and differentiated from other units. Equally important, this concept refers to how the unit defines the space where it exists by its properties and the interaction with other units. An organic structure is set to have continuous resources exchanges and coordination among all units and systems, so that the whole system works adequately. Organizationally speaking, the structure will be set and conditioned to reaffirm the identity of every unit and have it integrated to the rest of the system.

Life cycle: Organic organizations have life cycles like biological beings. They are born, grow, develop, some reproduce, and eventually die.

Trust: Since members of an organic structure will have the organic level of consciousness, there will be no need for enforcement of laws, rules, and regulations. People will be coordinated and not controlled. Units (people, teams, departments, etc.) will be aware of their responsibilities and the importance of fulfilling their tasks for the proper operation of the system. There will be no need for control over people, but rather *trust* that they will accomplish their missions.

Everyone will trust other members of the system, and will convey trust on others about their tasks.

Coordination: Hierarchy is a human convention created to organize a group of people to reach pre-established goals, by means of a structure of supervisors and staff. But, hierarchy is not widely found in biological systems (Boulding, 1953). Hierarchy has a different meaning in organic structures. It is not based on a bureaucratic structure, but rather on priorities based on fundamental values, like the survival of the system, or the system balanced operation. The organic hierarchy is based on the fulfillment of tasks and goals by units and systems, always having the general well-being as the top priority. No unit is subordinated to another unit by receiving instructions or being controlled. Every single unit fulfills its task autonomously, collaboratively, integrated and with solidarity, subordinating its own interest to the general well-being. Priorities are not based on instructions provided by supervisors, but on values and the general well-being. This may be accomplished by a conscious behavior of every unit - be it person, group, department or organization. The organic level of consciousness will guide every unit's behavior and actions towards the general well-being. All members' decisions will be respected in an organic organization, due to being originated from the organic conscious level. As part of this conceptualization, the traditional bureaucratic hierarchy will be replaced with *coordination of activities*, by means of an organizational structure that allows the best possible performance based on people's autonomy, freedom of action, rightful structure operation, and *member's conscious behavior*. Coordination of activities will be proportionally important with the amount of units and resources, to ensure the proper flow of information and decisions. A specific unit acting as the brain of the system will execute the coordination of activities. Its main function will be to coordinate the organic organization operation, ensuring that the required conditions are provided to every unit to accomplish their mission, and make sure they are properly integrated to the rest of the system.

Decentralization: Coordination and autonomy will drive the system operation to a level where functions can be performed without the supervision of a central authority.

Differentiation: The process by which cells or parts serve a specific function applies to organic organizational structures as well. Every unit has a specific function, which make up part of the whole functionality of the system.

Equifinality: A desired end state may be reached through different ways, depending on initial conditions, environment variables, and resources availability.

Flexibility: People and organic units can perform different tasks in different moments as part of their place in the system. The important thing is to provide the system with a service to reach the general well-being. The organic structure is flexible both in its nature and the tasks of its units, as long as the operation of the system is rightly fulfilled. Every unit should be flexible with regards to the task to be performed: it may change depending on the needs of the system.

Homeostasis: This is about the tendency towards a relatively stable equilibrium between interdependent units, especially as maintained by physiological processes. An organizational organic structure can modify its conditions of operation to adapt to a changing environment, just like the human body and biological beings do.

Integration: The proper operation of the system will depend on the capability of the units to be integrated and coordinated with the rest of the system, and the ability of becoming a whole.

Implicate order: every organic structure has an implicate order that rules the explicate order. "The laws of the implicate order are such that there is a relatively independent, recurrent, stable sub-totality which constitutes the explicate order, and which, of course, is basically the order that we commonly contact in common experience" (Bohm. 2002: 263). The explicate order is consequence of the implicate order. Modern sciences have reached fantastic levels of reality description - the explicate order -, providing understanding of causes and effects, but do not explain the implicated order, why everything happens this way. But the implicate order exists, and determine natural phenomena different manifestations. But, what is this implicate order? What rules the explicate order? The answer is that the **Universal implicate order is Love**, and everything else results from it. Human beings come from Love, this immeasurable force which gives rise to every form of life, organic and inorganic; bases the life flowing through human hearts; gives rise to the miracle of life; allows turning the impossible into possible; inspires thoughts, emotions, and consciousness; gives rise to the tangible and intangible, spiritual and eternal, visible and invisible manifestations; and provides reading, comprehension, and understanding of ideas and thoughts. This implicate order gives rise to eternal manifestations in the material dimension. The man will only manifest eternal values, harmony, and right actions by flowing with this wonderful force. The human race will only adopt principles and positions aligned with the Truth by recognizing and accepting the implicate order of Love as part of their essence. This will let flow what is true in human hearts and will give rise to a harmonious social order and collaborative organizational structures.

Leadership: Leadership is everywhere and anywhere in the system. This will based on every person and unit fulfilling their vocation, aware of their responsibility and contribution to the operation of the system, and attentive to any failure in order to be corrected. As with the human body, where the leadership is based on the *implicate order,* and every cell, tissue, organ and system "know" what to do for keeping the body working; similarly, people and units are responsible for fulfilling their corresponding tasks in the organic organization. Only under exceptional circumstances leadership may be based on one unit for a limited period. In this case, there might be the need of a *temporary unit* to lead the system to face an unexpected situation. This leader unit should be selected by consensus based on its expertise, experience, and capability of leading the system to make the right choices. The team members on their side will be conscious enough to understand the situation, and give up part of their leadership to follow the leader's decisions and proposals until the exceptional circumstances are over, or the system has adapted to new conditions. Then, everything will be back to normal. In the case of a similar situation on another area of expertise, the team may choose a different temporary leader by consensus.

Unity over time: The organic structure remains as a unit from birth until death. After this, all component parts will disaggregate and make up part of another system, not necessarily together or to the same destination[4]. Unity over time does not mean that all components will be strictly the same over the lifetime, but that the system will be composed of the same type of units. For example, the same organs and tissues integrate the human body, but their cells are renovated continuously[5].

3. ORGANIC FORCES

3.1 Organic Attraction Force

There is an attraction force existing in organic systems[6], which keeps them together during their lifetime. This is referred to as the *Organic Attraction Force.*

The attraction force is present in planetary systems by means of Gravity, which keeps them stable and compact. In the sub-atomic universe, the attraction force keeps electrons, protons, and neutrons within a circumscribed field, preserving atoms and molecules as units. In biological beings, the attraction force keeps bodies' components together, allowing them to stay as units.

---

[4]   After a living being death, all components (cells, tissues and organs) will disaggregate and make up part of another system (i.e. organic waste on the soil). The organic material is not destroyed, but separated and integrated to another system.

[5]   Similarly, an organization maintains its identity as long as it exists, even that people may be replaced with others for fulfilling the same tasks. If the organization closes (i.e. dies), ex-employees will go somewhere else.

[6]   This is related to any natural system that can be modelled as an organic structure.

The Organic Attraction Force is present on every system qualified as organic. Should this force disappears or vanish, this system will lose its identity as a unit; such as a dead biological being, an atomic fission, or a supernova (the explosion of a star).

Organizational and social systems have attraction forces as well. This is the natural force that keeps groups, organizations, companies or communities together. Members make up part of a given system, fulfill their tasks, or live in it as long as they belong to the system. This force keeps communities, towns, cities and countries together. Likewise for companies, organizations and institutions.

At some point, a member may decide to leave this group, organization, company or community to go to another one. But they will probably go to a similar system with its corresponding attraction force.

3.2 Organic Centrifugal Force

The organic attraction force is usually balanced by a force with same magnitude but opposite direction, called the *Organic Centrifugal Force*, which maintains the appropriate balance between attraction and repulsion.

Generally speaking, the Organic Centrifugal Force is related to the movement of the elements. In the case of planetary systems, it is generated by the movement of the planets that balances the gravity attraction to the Sun; in sub-atomic systems, the movements of the electrons prevent them from being attracted to the nucleus.

In the case of social and organizational systems, this force induces the existence of a *minimum vital space* required for employees to work comfortably, or people to live at ease in their communities. When this minimum vital space is not respected, conflicts arise in the workplace, and people's behavior tends to be aggressive against their peers.

3.3 Balance and Vital Space of Organic Systems

Both forces coexist and balance mutually to shape organic systems. The movement of the planets balances the gravity attraction force, thus shaping the solar system; the movement of electrons counterbalances the nucleus attraction force, thus shaping atoms and molecules; cells, tissues and organs maintain a balanced system, thus shaping biological beings; and people live and work together, but maintaining their space and individuality.

The Attraction Force depends usually on the essence of the organic units (electromagnetism, gravity, biological balance, and/or people's necessity to be related), while the Centrifugal Force depends usually on the organic units movement. The Attraction Force is usually static, while the Centrifugal Force is dynamic.

A balance between these two forces creates the *Vital Space*, which shows the organic units necessity of a minimum physical space, be it atoms, cells, living beings, organizations, communities or planets.

The attraction and centrifugal forces have not been formally stated yet at organizational and social levels, but they exist. The attraction force manifests itself as the necessity of people to be with other people, either physically, or in a moral situation of having the same ideas (Fromm, 1952). The centrifugal force manifests itself by means of every person preserving his identity and necessity to differentiate from others.

From social and organizational standpoints, both forces translate into a balance, not necessarily harmonious, which shapes and provides life to social and organizational systems. Not necessarily harmonious means that conflict frequently exists in organizations and social systems, due mainly to an imbalance between both forces, and *Vital Space* transgression. It is well-known how big cities boost conflict between people, either in a traffic jam or walking in the downtown. Incidentally, a strange phenomenon comes up when the population density is high: people are less willing to meet with others or share with them. The transgression of their vital space due to the population density makes people withdraw into themselves, in order to preserve their vital space.

The imbalance between both forces boosts conflict in social systems. *Individualism* (imbalance due to a stronger attraction force, where every individual considers his well-being more important than others') reinforces the predominance of the individual over the group, and creates conflicts between individuals, each one of them fighting for his own well-being, driving behaviors in different directions within the system. This provides the ideal breeding ground for the emergence of conflicts in a social system, every person acting differently and divergently with respect to each other. When someone considers he is more important than others, he tends to underestimate them, considers his well-being more important, and sets the well-being of others in a lower level of priorities. Thus, he will not pay attention their necessities, and conflicts will rise in his personal, organizational and social relationships.

Let us try to see what individualism could do in the human body. Let us assume that every organ is individualistic, that the heart pumps must of the blood for itself, and that every organ does the same. How long would the human body survive? Not long for sure.

On the other side, *collectivism* (imbalance due to a stronger centrifugal force) prioritizes the group over each individual, driving actions and efforts to others well-being. When someone considers others' well-being more important than his, his well-being becomes subordinated to that of others', and he will always put his well-being second on the level of priorities. He may forget that his well-being is as important as others', and that he needs to be well to help others. This creates an imbalance on his social entourage.

In the case of the human body, would it be possible for it to function properly if every organ worked only for the others, without giving itself part of their own task? Likewise, it would not live long. Every organ should work for itself and the others, to ensure the human body's balance, and thus its survival.

Balance is essential between both forces to preserve the existence of every organic system.

This same approach can be applied to social and organizational systems, where balance is absolutely necessary for creating harmonious systems, and driving people's behavior towards a common goal.

Equilibrium between individuals and the system should exist so that every member can find within himself the necessity to direct his efforts to achieve his well-being and that of others. If every single member of an organization acts this way, harmony would certainly replace conflict in any system.

Imbalanced situations discourage the continuity of the system. On one side, *Individualism* is implosive, making the service members can provide to the system decrease over time. On the other side, *Collectivism* is dispersive, disaggregates the system, makes members focus their actions towards others, and decreases social systems cohesion. *A balanced situation in a social system is based on member's behavior where each one's well-being is as important as others'. This makes conflict decrease, and be replaced by harmony in social interactions.*

Balance is mostly related to the respect of vital space, which will allow us to create a harmonious system. Vital space is not only related to physical space, but to other conditions as well, that should be fulfilled to ensure the right development of a person or a social system, such as autonomy, decision-making power, freedom of action, and vocation exercising. Every person and social system should be provided with a minimum vital space to fulfill their tasks. If the vital space is not respected, conflict arises almost immediately in organizational and social systems. Consequences of this may be disastrous for the system operation: member's discomfort, productivity decrease, roles and responsibilities conflicts, excessive hierarchical control, lack of power of decision-making, communication issues, and discontinuous flow of resources.

A balance between the organic forces and the respect of the vital space are of paramount importance for designing harmonious organizational and social structures. This will result in members acting for the general well-being, and social structures where individuals, groups, organizations, and communities will develop at their highest level.

4. ORGANIZATIONAL MODELING: DEGREE OF ORGANICITY

"In many phenomena in biology and also in the behavioral and social sciences, mathematical expressions are applicable"

Ludwig Von Bertalanffy

This section is intended for organizational modeling only, through the use of matrices. It can be skipped by those who are not interested in this area.

The *degree of organicity* will refer to the proximity of an organizational structure to organic systems functionality. The higher the level of organicity, the more similar an organization operation will be to organic systems. For this purpose, the matrix format will be used to represent organizational structures.

4.1 The Matrix Representation of an Organizational Structure

Organizational structures will be described as matrices, where units, relationships between units, and the structure can be represented.

Let us assume that there is a structure comprised of n-units, each one noted as a_i (i= 1, 2... n). Each unit a_i can relate to another unit a_j (j= 1, 2... n -1). This relationship will be noted as a_{ij}, which means "relationship between unit i and unit j". This relationship will have one of the following values:

a_{ij} = 0, if relationship of unit i with unit j harms unit j. This type of relationship will be called *non-cooperative.*

a_{ij} = 1, if relationship of unit i with unit j benefits unit j, or at least does not harm j. This type of relationship will be called *cooperative.*

Clarifications:

- In affirming that a unit harms another unit, we refer to a relationship where the operation of this unit damages the operation of the second unit. For example: a cancer cell harms the functionality of surrounding cells. Thus, the relationship between this cell with the rest of the cells will be noted as "0".

- In affirming that a unit benefits another unit, we refer to a relationship where the operation of this unit supports the operation of the second unit. Or at least, it does not harm it.

The relationship between all units a_{ij} (i= 1, 2... n; j= 1, 2... n) operating in a net-structure will be represented as a matrix, where the unit a_{ii} (i=j) will be the relationship of a unit with itself, and its value will be 1 by definition.

Net-structure matrix A_{ij} of n-units (i= 1, 2... n; j= 1, 2... n) will be represented as follows:

$$A_{nn} = \begin{vmatrix} a_{11} & a_{12} & a_{13} & \cdots & a_{1n} \\ a_{21} & a_{22} & \cdots & & a_{2n} \\ \cdot & \cdot & & & \cdot \\ \cdot & & \cdot & & \cdot \\ \cdot & & & \cdot & \\ a_{n1} & a_{n2} & \cdots & & a_{nn} \end{vmatrix}$$

In this matrix, elements values are either 0 or 1, which represent the relationship between each unit with the rest of the units. Relationships a_{ij} and a_{ji} will not necessarily be the same, because unit "i" may harm unit "j", but unit "j" may be providing support to unit "i". For example, a cancer cell can cause harm to a healthy cell, but the healthy cell may be providing support to the cancer cell. In this case, if we define the cancer cell as a_1, and normal cell as a_2, a_{12} will be equal to 0 ($a_{12} = 0$), which represents the relationship of the cancer cell with the normal cell, and a_{21} will be equal to 1 ($a_{21} = 1$), which represents the relationship of the normal cell with the cancer cell.

This relationship matrix can be represented as follows:

$$A_{22} = \begin{vmatrix} a_{11} & a_{12} \\ a_{21} & a_{22} \end{vmatrix} \Rightarrow A_{22} = \begin{vmatrix} 1 & 0 \\ 1 & 1 \end{vmatrix}$$

As we can see, matrix A_{22} is not symmetrical ($a_{12} \neq a_{21}$)

4.2 Definitions

Definition 1: *The relationship of a unit with itself will be cooperative* $(a_{ij} = 1$, *when* $i = j$; $a_{11} = a_{22} = a_{33} = a_{44} = \ldots = a_{nn} = 1)$.

This will be called harmonious individual principle: a unit will support its own operation and development, and will not harm itself.

Definition 2: *A net-structure is composed by inter-connected similar units willing to work together.*

We would like to highlight the term "willing to" in this definition. This represents the units' capability of working together, but it is not mandatory. Conditions are set to do so, but this is not guaranteed. Another term to highlight is "similar", due to the fact that units are defined as equals.

Definition 3: *A net-structure will be considered an "Individualistic Structure", if and only if, all values in matrix* A_{nn} *are equal to zero (0), except for those that should be equal to one by definition 1.*

The Individualistic Structure establishes that every unit acts only for its own benefit, and harms other units operation. The matrix representation is as follows:

$$A_{nn} = \begin{vmatrix} 1 & 0 & 0 & \ldots & 0 \\ 0 & 1 & 0 & & 0 \\ 0 & 0 & 1 & & . \\ . & & . & & . \\ . & & & . & \\ 0 & 0 & \ldots & & 1 \end{vmatrix}$$

Definition 4: A net-structure will be called "Collaborative Structure", if at least two mutual given values (a_{ij} e a_{ji}) are equal to one (1).

It is sufficient that at least two units collaborate with each other to confirm the collaborative nature of a net-structure.

Definition 5: A net-structure will be called "Harmonious Structure", if and only if, all values in matrix A_{nn} are equal to one (1).

The Harmonious Structure establishes that all units collaborate with each other, supporting both their own benefits and others'. The matrix representation will be:

$$
A_{nn} = \begin{vmatrix}
1 & 1 & 1 & \cdots & 1 \\
1 & 1 & 1 & & 1 \\
1 & 1 & 1 & & . \\
. & & & & . \\
. & & & . & \\
1 & 1 & \cdots & & 1
\end{vmatrix}
$$

4.3 Degree of Organicity

The degree of organicity depends on the ration of values equal to 1. The maximum possible number of values equal to 1 of an organizational structure will be the square of the number of members.

Let us say there is an organizational structure of 4 members, with the following values:

$$A_{44} = \begin{vmatrix} 1 & 1 & 1 & 1 \\ 1 & 1 & 1 & 0 \\ 1 & 0 & 1 & 1 \\ 0 & 1 & 0 & 1 \end{vmatrix}$$

In this case, twelve (12) values are equal to 1, and four (4) values equal to 0. Then, *the degree of organicity of this structure will be 75%,* which results from dividing the number of values equal to 1 (12) by the total elements of the matrix (16): 12/16 x 100 = 75%.

The higher the ratio of values equals to 1, the higher the degree of organicity of an organizational structure, and vice versa.

4.4 Diverse types of Organizational Matrixes

A few examples of organizational structures will be detailed as follows:

a) Cases of two people collaborating and two people competing

Two people will be represented as a_1 and a_2. Relationships will be a_{11}, a_{22}, a_{21} and a_{12}. Values of a_{11} and a_{22} are equal to one (1) by definition. Values of a_{12} and a_{21} represent the relationship of 1 to 2, and vice versa.

- The matrix representation will be:

$$A_{22} = \begin{vmatrix} a_{11} & a_{12} \\ a_{21} & a_{22} \end{vmatrix}$$

- The graphic representation will be one of the following three cases:

1) Case 1:

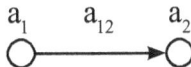

The arrow representation means a collaborative relationship from a_1 to a_2 ($a_{12} = 1$), but not the opposite ($a_{21} = 0$).

2) Case 2:

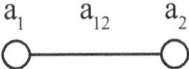

A straight line means no collaboration from a_1 to a_2, and vice versa ($a_{12} = a_{21} = 0$).

3) Case 3:

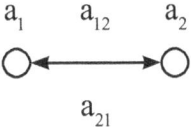

A double arrow means mutual collaborative relationship ($a_{12} = a_{21} = 1$).

a.1) Two people do not collaborate with each other, a_{12} and a_{21} values will be:

$a_{12} = 0$ (a_1 does not collaborate with a_2)
$a_{21} = 0$ (a_2 does not collaborate with a_1)

And, by definition: $a_{11} = a_{22} = 1$ (each one collaborates with himself)

- The matrix representation will be the individualistic matrix 2 x 2:

$$A_{22} = \begin{vmatrix} 1 & 0 \\ 0 & 1 \end{vmatrix}$$

- The graphic representation will be:

$\Rightarrow$ When two people's behavior is individualistic, they are isolated from each other, and there is not a net-structure.

a.2) Two people collaborate with each other, a_{12} and a_{21} values will be:

$a_{12} = 1$ (a_1 collaborate with a_2)
$a_{21} = 1$ (a_2 collaborate with a_1)

And, by definition: $a_{11} = a_{22} = 1$ (each one collaborates with himself)

- The matrix representation will be the harmonious matrix 2 x 2:

$$A_{22} = \begin{vmatrix} 1 & 1 \\ 1 & 1 \end{vmatrix}$$

- The graphic representation will be:

$\Rightarrow$ When two people collaborate with each other, they benefit each other. There is a net-structure.

a.3) One person collaborates with the second person, but the second person does not collaborate, a_{12} and a_{21} values will be:

$a_{12} = 1$ (a_1 collaborate with a_2)
$a_{21} = 0$ (a_2 does not collaborate with a_1)

And, by definition: $a_{11} = a_{22} = 1$ (each one collaborates with himself)

- Matrix representation:

$$A_{22} = \begin{vmatrix} 1 & 1 \\ 0 & 1 \end{vmatrix}$$

- Graphic representation:

⇒ When only one person collaborates, the net-structure functionality becomes incomplete.

b) Three people acting together – competitive and collaborative cases

Three people are represented as a_1, a_2 and a_3. The relationships between them will be a_{11}, a_{12}, a_{13}, a_{21}, a_{22}, a_{23}, a_{31}, a_{32} and a_{33}. Values a_{11}, a_{22} and a_{33} will be equal to 1 by definition. Other values will depend on the relationship.

- Matrix representation:

$$A_{33} = \begin{vmatrix} a_{11} & a_{12} & a_{13} \\ a_{21} & a_{22} & a_{23} \\ a_{31} & a_{32} & a_{33} \end{vmatrix}$$

- Graphic representation:

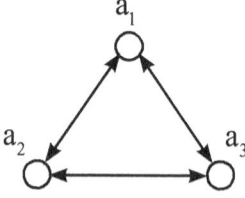

b.1) Three people's behaviors are individualistic. Values will be as follows:

$a_{12} = a_{13} = a_{21} = a_{23} = a_{31} = a_{32} = 0$ (no collaboration between members)

$a_{11} = a_{22} = a_{33} = 1$ (each one collaborates with himself)

- Matrix representation:

$$A_{33} = \begin{vmatrix} 1 & 0 & 0 \\ 0 & 1 & 0 \\ 0 & 0 & 1 \end{vmatrix}$$

- Graphic representation:

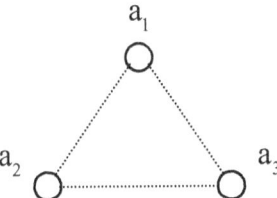

$\Rightarrow$ When three people's behavior is individualistic, they act isolated from each other. There is no net-structure.

b.2) Three people collaborating. Values will be:

$a_{12} = a_{13} = a_{21} = a_{23} = a_{31} = a_{32} = 1$ (collaboration between a_1, a_2 and a_3)

$a_{11} = a_{22} = a_{33} = 1$

- Matrix representation – the harmonious matrix:

$$A_{33} = \begin{vmatrix} 1 & 1 & 1 \\ 1 & 1 & 1 \\ 1 & 1 & 1 \end{vmatrix}$$

- Graphic representation:

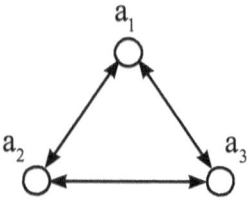

⇒ When three members collaborate with each other, they benefit others and the structure functionality. There is a complete *net-structure*.

b.3) Two collaborate with each other (a_1 and a_2), but the third one (a_3) is individualistic. Values will be:

$a_{12} = a_{21} = 1$ (a_1 and a_2 collaborating with each other)

$a_{13} = a_{23} = a_{31} = a_{32} = 0$ (a_3 does not collaborate with a_1 and a_2)

- Matrix representation:

$$A_{33} = \begin{vmatrix} 1 & 1 & 0 \\ 1 & 1 & 0 \\ 0 & 0 & 1 \end{vmatrix}$$

- Graphic representation:

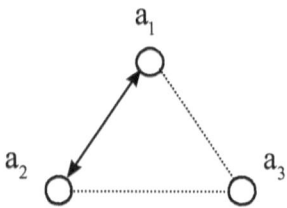

⇒ When two members collaborate with each other, some benefit from others, but not all of them. This is an incomplete *net-structure*.

Two people collaborating with each other formalize the net-structure, though incomplete, due to the individualistic behavior of the third member.

4.5 The Representation of Hierarchy

Two simple cases of hierarchical structures follow:

a) Case of non cooperative hierarchy

This case represents a situation where the supervisor benefits from the employees work but he does not cooperate with them. For their part, employees cooperate with their supervisor, but not all of them cooperate with each other.

Members of this team: three employees (a_1, a_2, and a_3) and supervisor (a_4). Employee a_1 cooperates with a_1 and a_3, and supervisor a_4. Employee a_2 does not cooperate with a_1, but cooperates with a_3 and the supervisor. Employee a_3 does not cooperate with a_1 and a_2, but only with the supervisor. The supervisor does not cooperate with any of the employees, but only with himself. Values will be:

$a_{11} = 1$ (a_1 cooperates with himself) $a_{21} = 0$ (a_2 does not cooperate with a_1)
$a_{12} = 1$ (a_1 cooperates with a_2) $a_{22} = 1$ (a_2 cooperates with himself)
$a_{13} = 1$ (a_1 cooperates with a_3) $a_{23} = 1$ (a_2 cooperates with a_3)
$a_{14} = 1$ (a_1 cooperates with the supervisor) $a_{24} = 1$ (a_2 cooperates with the supervisor)

$a_{31} = 0$ (a_3 does not cooperate with a_1) $a_{41} = 0$ (supervisor does not cooperates with a_1)

$a_{32} = 0$ (a_3 does not cooperate with a_2) $a_{42} = 0$ (supervisor does not cooperate w/ a_2)

$a_{33} = 1$ (a_3 cooperates with himself) $a_{43} = 0$ (supervisor does not cooperate w/ a_3)

$a_{34} = 1$ (a_3 cooperates with the supervisor) $a_{44} = 1$ (supervisor cooperates with himself)

- Matrix representation:

$$A_{44} = \begin{vmatrix} a_{11} & a_{12} & a_{13} & a_{14} \\ a_{21} & a_{22} & a_{23} & a_{24} \\ a_{31} & a_{32} & a_{33} & a_{34} \\ a_{41} & a_{42} & a_{43} & a_{44} \end{vmatrix} \Rightarrow A_{44} = \begin{vmatrix} 1 & 1 & 1 & 1 \\ 0 & 1 & 1 & 1 \\ 0 & 0 & 1 & 1 \\ 0 & 0 & 0 & 1 \end{vmatrix}$$

- Graphic representation:

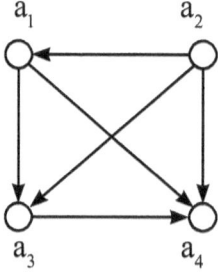

a_1 a_2

a_3 a_4

Note: There is no double arrow present, which means there is no reciprocal cooperation between any of the units

⇒ This result shows a hierarchical organization based on non-cooperative units. They represent a structure where most of the units are acting separately. All units' behaviors are individualistic. None of these units cooperates reciprocally with any of the other units (no double arrow). Practically speaking, there is an incomplete net-structure.

b) Case of hierarchy with tendency to cooperate

This case represents a hierarchical situation where at least two units cooperate with each other (i.e. two employees, or supervisor plus an employee).

Members of this team: three employees (a_1, a_2, and a_3) and supervisor (a_4). Employee a_1 cooperates with a_2 and a_3, and supervisor a_4. Employee a_2 cooperates with a_1, a_3 and the supervisor. Employee a_3 does not cooperate with a_1 and a_2, but only with the supervisor. The supervisor cooperates with a_1 and a_2, but not with a_3. Values are:

$a_{11} = 1$ (a_1 cooperates with himself) $a_{21} = 1$ (a_2 cooperates with a_1)
$a_{12} = 1$ (a_1 cooperates with a_2) $a_{22} = 1$ (a_2 cooperates with himself)
$a_{13} = 1$ (a_1 cooperates with a_3) $a_{23} = 1$ (a_2 cooperates with a_3)
$a_{14} = 1$ (a_1 cooperates with supervisor) $a_{24} = 1$ (a_2 cooperates with supervisor)

$a_{31} = 0$ (a_3 does not cooperate with a_1) $a_{41} = 1$ (supervisor cooperates with a_1)
$a_{32} = 0$ (a_3 does not cooperate with a_2) $a_{42} = 1$ (supervisor cooperates with con a_2)
$a_{33} = 1$ (a_3 cooperates with himself) $a_{43} = 0$ (supervisor does not cooperate with a_3)
$a_{34} = 1$ (a_3 cooperates with supervisor) $a_{44} = 1$ (supervisor cooperates with himself)

- Matrix representation:

$$A_{44} = \begin{vmatrix} a_{11} & a_{12} & a_{13} & a_{14} \\ a_{21} & a_{22} & a_{23} & a_{24} \\ a_{31} & a_{32} & a_{33} & a_{34} \\ a_{41} & a_{42} & a_{43} & a_{44} \end{vmatrix} \Rightarrow A_{44} = \begin{vmatrix} 1 & 1 & 1 & 1 \\ 1 & 1 & 1 & 1 \\ 0 & 0 & 1 & 1 \\ 1 & 1 & 0 & 1 \end{vmatrix}$$

- Graphic representation:

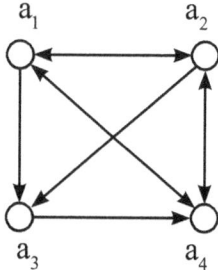

a_1 a_2

a_3 a_4

Note: There are three double arrows – reciprocal cooperation between three units

$\Rightarrow$ A hierarchical organization with tendency to cooperate makes the net-structure, due to two units cooperating reciprocally.

4.6 Partial Conclusions

Same analysis can be applied to matrix structures with more units. Our conclusions for up to 10 units are as follows:

1) Hierarchy does not make much sense in a net-structure. The important fact is cooperation between units, and not the value

added by the supervisor. Additionally, cooperation enables the emergence of synergy, where the effect of units working together is greater than the sum of their separate effects.

2) The "net-structure" term cannot be applied to an individualistic matrix structure, but to a system where at least two units are collaborating with each other.

3) The more units support each other, the higher the level of *organicity* of the net-structure. Thus, the closer its functionality to natural organic structures.

The organic paradigm guidelines have been established at social and organizational levels. We will review its application to a large scale in the next chapter: the Organic Society.

CHAPTER 3

THE ORGANIC SOCIETY

The Organic Society approach is structured in three clearly differentiated parts: the organization of work, the organic economy, and organic communities; all of them decisive aspects of harmonious and collaborative social systems.

1. THE ORGANIZATION OF WORK

The organization of work is fundamental in every social system. Some suggestions have surfaced in this essay about how work may be organized. For example, hierarchy and control mechanisms should be replaced with coordination and conscious behaviors; and production and service units should be organized as net-structures. However, further discussion is required to better outline the organic proposal.

At the present time, the following topics make up part of the labor agenda in many countries: structural unemployment, substitution of technology with manpower, reduction of working day hours to preserve employment, and developing countries competitiveness due to reduced cost of labor. These issues are usually tackled by measures set by a government, which result in only partial success and they tend not to be entirely satisfactory for all parts involved. This is due to the limitations of current modern society paradigms.

The implementation of a governmental measure aiming to tackle a labor market issue is followed by a collateral effect, which reduces the expected effect of this measure. By way of illustration, the employment insurance, which aims to keep the unemployed in the consumer market while looking for a job, has the collateral effect of people working informally and enjoying the unemployment insurance at the same time. This represents a deviation from the main goal, which is to provide financial support while looking for a job.

Collateral effects are usually tackled with additional governmental measures, which have other collateral effects, and so on. This frequently become a vicious cycle, *resulting from the rational and fragmented analysis of reality.*

A different perspective should be assumed to analyze reality, not only about the labor market, but social reality in general. This should be based on a specific analysis of a given situation accompanied with a global view, in order to take the appropriate measures. Reality should be viewed differently.

1.1 Inclusion of Technology into Work

Current Perspective

Since the beginning of the Second Industrial Revolution, the inclusion of technology into the production system has always been seen as a threat to employment and the cause of employee migration.

Every new technology included in the production system tends to replace people in routine activities, specifically those where machines can perform repetitive tasks. From the point of view of the person being replaced, this can be a relief as long as he does not lose his job and simultaneously is trained to perform another task, thus preventing him from performing a task that is not providing any sort of personal fulfillment, other than having an income for living. From the economic theory perspective, technological innovation enables economic prosperity, because it increases productivity, reduces production costs, improves the quality of products, and makes employees migrate to other industries where manpower may be required.

At the present time, production systems tend to innovate through automation, where employees supervise production processes and machines execute the physical work more and more.

However, because of the rapid rate of current technological innovation, the job creation rate may not keep up with the pace to compensate the loss of jobs. Therefore, this is causing a *structural unemployment*.

Current conflicting modern societies paradigms are making this happen: people need to work to have an income, be part of the economic system and enjoy its benefits. But, on the other hand, people are being replaced with automatic systems, which make them lose their jobs and corresponding income.

Current modern paradigms show inconsistencies: people need to work to have an income, but they are being replaced within an economic system, that is unable to create enough jobs to absorb them. Thus, some of the replaced people face a situation where they are not part of the system, nor have an income to make up part of the *included*; and those who are *excluded* enjoy only a temporary unemployment income. But exclusion tends to grow. How many unemployed can a social system stand?

Modern societies suffer from two additional inconsistencies of equal importance:

a) Technological innovation increases productivity, so that more products and services are available to consumers; but more and more people are unable to purchase them, thus the unemployed are increasingly becoming excluded.

b) Technological innovation prevents people from performing routine and repetitive activities, which hypothetically will allow them to work on tasks more oriented to personal fulfillment, but, the economic system demands people to find a job, independently if it is routine or repetitive.

Industrial societies are not dealing properly with people being replaced with automatic systems, to adapt to new circumstances where people are not part of the production system, but could still work towards their personal fulfillment.

We live within a technology inclusion system that does not respond to questions related to the availability of a replaced person. Technological inclusion increases productivity, and decreases routine activities for employees, but does not provide answers to the people who are replaced. Modern societies benefit from technological inclusion to produce more products and services with better quality; but does not provide solutions to the availability of the displaced persons, to their personal fulfillment, or to their income after they are replaced.

Current economic system paradigms do not provide solutions to people being replaced with technology, nor take advantage of their availability for performing non-productive activities.

Machines will do most of the work at some point in the future, and human participation will be reduced to a minimal expression. Then, what will the economic system do with all products, services and people availability?

Organic Perspective

The organic approach deals with the role of work in Society, and the people's desire of fulfilment.

Any social system can be considered an organic structure. As such, some members' well-being should not be disregarded to support that of others; nor compromise a few members' benefits to give them to others; or even, cannot justify that some barely fulfill their needs, while others have more than they need to live. The organic perspective does not divide social system members between main beneficiaries and underprivileged. All members should be equally treated, and their well-being equally important.

Can we imagine a human body where only two or three organs receive most of the nutrients from the ingested food, whereas the rest of the organs only receive the minimum for survival? Can we visualize a body where only one part (i.e. leg) grows healthy, and the rest stay under famine conditions? This is hard to imagine. We all consider the human body as a unit, and see it as an organic structure where all parts should reap the benefits of the system equally.

Every member is equally important for the system under the organic perspective. If the system benefits from economic growth, all members should enjoy this gain; but, if there is a recession, all members should share the loss equally. All members make up part of the system. The well-being of the social system and of all members are intrinsically connected.

1) Role of work

As part of the organic approach, work is the way to provide the Society with a service, and gives the right to enjoy the fruits of others' work. Work should be the vehicle by which someone manifests his vocation and fulfills his dreams. Work allows a conscious man to provide his contribution to Society and to the well-being of others. Every member will be both a service provider and a receiver. When someone provides a service to the system, he provides to himself the right to receive from others.

Work will not be viewed as a burden to individuals for surviving, but as a means to enable their personal fulfillment, coming fundamentally from two ways: by working on their vocation, thus, enjoying what they do for living; and the awareness of providing the Society with a service.

Every member needs clothes, food, dwelling, material objects, and service from others for living. The main goal of an economic system is to organize the products and services production/ distribution so that all members meet their needs *freely, equally, fairly and consciously. Freely,* to ensure that products and services are easily accessible to all; *equally,* because every member has the same rights and duties; *fairly,* to ensure that everyone gets what they need; and *consciously,* because everyone will not get more than required to meet their needs.

2) Inclusion of Technology

The inclusion of technology to replace people in routine and repetitive activities should provide them with extra time to be allocated for their personal fulfillment. This will allow them to work on their vocation for the Society well-being, rather than executing a repetitive activity that does not add value to their personal growth. Technology can set people free of repetitive meaningless activities, in order to provide them with other type of activities aligned with their personal growth.

Personal fulfillment includes any type of activity that makes people feel alive, and that makes them think that their lives make sense. *This comprises any type activity where people's hearts are involved.* In other words, *any type of activity performed with passion,* be it research, non-profit, sports, arts, writing, teaching, crafts, day to day work, etc.

Technology inclusion can make all Society members' material needs be met, including those who do not perform any productive activity. Technology can increase production as much as needed to fulfill people's material requirements, without limitations imposed by economic models paradigms, like market, price, costs, profit, and efficiency. *Production can increase until people's needs are completely satisfied.*

3) Vocation

Conscious citizens find their personal fulfillment by meeting their needs, performing their vocation, providing the Society with a service, helping others to meet their needs, and growing continuously both personally and spiritually.

Motivation is an important factor for performing a job in the Organic Society. *Only an individual who is performing his vocation can be continuously motivated.* Other than being suited, trained, or qualified, vocation is based mostly in the Heart, on what someone likes to do, the passion he feels when he is working in his field/area, and the task where he feels most comfortable to provide others with his service.

Since technology is replacing manpower in many activities, at some point many people will have time available to perform their vocation. But, there may be some activities not fully automated, where human tasks may still be needed. In this case, conscious citizens will offer part of their time to perform these type of tasks, on a rotational basis by all members of the social system. Thus, there will be two types of rotation: every member will rotate between his vocation and activities not fully automated; and, all suitable members will rotate to perform these activities, within a dynamic where consciousness and solidarity will shape the social system functionality.

All people should have the right to perform their vocation, unless they decide consciously to do otherwise, due to help needed in other areas. For example, when technology is not enough to replace manpower for given production processes or services offered.

As for vocation, how can this be determined by every individual? People's vocation should be determined based on an educational process aiming to identify each individual's natural skills and personal choices since they enter the school system; not by the system needs, but what they love to perform. This way, their vocation can be identified at an early age, so that they will be able to perform their vocation at the working age, based on the passion for what they do, liberty of choice, consciousness, and personal skills.

4) Distribution

The income distribution should now be addressed, after having outlined the role of work, inclusion of technology and vocation.

The organic perspective states that there should be no income distinction among people, neither by type of job, nor by intellectual level required to complete tasks, or any other rational justification. Every member should have the same rights and duties, because the system needs all of them to perform their task properly, without any kind of differentiation. Even an individual, who performs a high technological or intellectual complex job, still needs every other member of the system to meet his needs.

The following conventions will shape the income distribution in an Organic system:

- Every Organic Society member is a conscious individual who works for his well-being and that of others.
- All members have the right meet their material needs and have a decent life.
- The economic priority is not the profit, but the free, equal, fair and conscious supply of products and services.

Based on these conventions, it is feasible to create an egalitarian distribution system of products and services within an organic social structure. Inequality should not be accepted due to ideological reasons, economic efficiency, or technological inclusion; only if someone consciously decides to surrender part of his material rights to give them to someone in need, due to humanitarian reasons. *This exception will come based on someone's level of consciousness, voluntary choice, and not on an economic system condition or limitation.*

5) The Consciousness of what is necessary

A conscious citizen will not try to get more than what he needs for living. Aware of his rights and responsibilities, he will be provided with all products and services required to have a decent life, and with the opportunity to provide others with a service. But he will not get more than what he needs, nor will he accumulate goods unnecessarily. The consciousness of what is necessary will prevent the system from producing more goods and services than is required to meet people's needs.

On the supply side, people's consciousness will set up a system where they will not work more than the necessary time to provide his service to the general well-being. In other words, *a system will be set up where the working time will not be ruled by a minimum amount of working hours per day or week, but by the lesser of the minimum working hours per day or week and what is necessary to reach the required production levels.*

Every member's working time will not be ruled by a pre-determined number of hours per day, or per week, but by the amount of time they need to finish their tasks. This will be established based on the time someone needs to provide the Society with his service, which will always be guided by a balance between his well-being and that of others. He should not have to work 8 hours or more per day, if he finishes his duty faster. There may be some exceptions in the case someone wants to work more than 8 hours per day. But as mentioned before, this amount of time should not be harmful to his health or well-being.

6) Organization of the Production System

The production system will be based on networked Organic Communities, set up properly to meet the Society's need for products and services.

An information system will have to be put in place to organize production and distribution systems, so that the market economy's "Price System" can be replaced. Other issues to be tackled by the organic production system are: productivity increase, technological innovation drivers, and efficiency improvement. The general principles of the *Organic Economy* follow.

2. THE ORGANIC ECONOMY

The *Organic Economy* will represent an alternative to the market economy. This will be based on a production system designed to meet demand, and a fair distribution system to allocate goods and services equally. Values such as cooperation and conscious behavior will be included in the design of this system.

2.1 Inefficiency of the Market's Economy

The main driver in a market economy is the *profit*, which arises from the self-interest of economic agents; the fundamental incentive is *their own necessities and satisfaction*; and the ultimate mechanism is the *competition*, which determines the level of production and distribution of goods and services on a large scale.

The market economy is a socioeconomic order emerged in the XIX century that subjugates men to the sale and purchase of goods. Today, practically everything can be sold and purchased. The origin of this oppression is the imposition of the capitalist system under the spectre of hunger, rather than inviting human beings to follow their natural trends (Polanyi. 1947).

The self-interest is not necessarily the right representation of the man. Therefore, it is no longer justifiable the imposition of a totalitarian economic system which nullifies the possibility of an alternative (Marcuse. 1973).

Polanyi affirms that "scanning the history of human civilization we do not find man acting so as to safeguard his individual interest in the acquisition of material goods, but rather to ensure his social standing, his social claims, his social assets" (Polanyi. 1947: 98). This questions the man's behavior as being essentially individualistic.

As for competition, this phenomenon occurs "whenever the resources or raw materials necessary for synthesis, growth or survival, are limited or become scarce" (Nicolis, Prigogine. 1977: 429). This questions *the competition* as a normal condition, one of the icons of the market economy. It is widely assumed, or even promoted, a general scarcity of products and services to ensure that the market economy works. There will never be enough products and services to satisfy all people's needs. The market economy production system regulates itself to reduce production until it reaches the profit level.

Competition and man's *self-interest* paradigms make sense in very specific situations. But they have been overestimated in current economic systems to achieve overall prosperity. Additionally, they have been used by powerful economic and political groups to ensure their own prosperity. These paradigms have turned into widely spread conventions, which maintain production and distribution systems to a large scale, but they ignore important human values such as equality, fairness, justice, cooperation and solidarity among people.

The market economy basis is that resources are scarce and man is individualistic, to set up massive production and distribution systems of goods and services, but unable to ensure that all members are provided equally with them. Therefore, these convenient conventions, but not necessarily true, support production and distribution systems, where fundamental human values are usually ignored, such as cooperation and solidarity.

As for the unequal distribution of wealth and resources, this may be due to one of the following factors: either the production level is not high enough to meet demand; or, production is at the right level, but goods are not distributed properly. From an ethical standpoint, both situations are unacceptable. There are no reasons not to produce at the right level, or distribute goods to meet demand. If a system should justify inequality for its proper functionality, then this system should be questioned, modified, or simply replaced.

If we could demonstrate that resources or raw materials levels are high enough to meet the world's population demand, then the market economy would have to be replaced by another type of system to ensure the right allocation of goods and services. Since this is out of the scope of the present essay, we will find support in our search for a different economic system, in an essay that shows the inefficiency of current economic systems to prevent hunger, even in the presence of enough food. Drèze and Sen[7], after analyzing the different causes of hunger in various parts of the planet Sub-Saharan Africa, Asia, and Latin America, affirmed that:

> "A person can be reduced to starvation if some economics change makes it no longer possible for him or her to acquire any commodity bundle with enough food. This can happen either because of a fall in endowment (e.g. alienation of land, or loss of labour power due to ill health), or because of an unfavourable shift in the condition of exchange (e.g. loss of

[7] Amartya Sen is an Indian economist and philosopher who received the 1998 Nobel Memorial Prize in Economic Sciences.
Jean Drèze is a Belgian-born Indian development economist who has been influential in the economic policy making of his country.

employment, fall in wages, rise in food prices, drop in the price of goods or services sold by the person, reduction of the social security provisions)" (Drèze and Sen. 1990: 3).

All above factors are related to the economic system organization. Then, they add:

"It is easy to establish that the acquirement problem is really central to questions of hunger and starvation in the modern world" (Drèze e Sen. 1990: 34-35)

Drèze and Sen show that food growth rate has outpaced the population growth rate (as per FAO[8], 1985), but hunger has increased in various parts of the world.

Current economic systems are inefficient to allocate resources equally. The man is subject to a permanent illusion of scarcity or resources to ensure that the system works efficiently, even if more resources are available.

Actually, the economic system ensures that the production decreases when there is plenty of resources, by means of price reduction, profit decrease, or producers going out of the market. *These regulation mechanisms do not allow the products and services allocation to all in need, but only to those who can afford them.*

---

[8]   FAO: Food and Agriculture Organization of the United Nations.

2.2 The Organic Economy

1) The Organic Incentive: Consciousness

The Organic Society members' behavior incentive will be their organic level of consciousness, which will ensure that all members take care of their own needs, and that of others. Since an individual with the organic level of consciousness considers others as part of himself, he considers the well-being of others part of his.

In this respect, a social system made up of people having the organic level of consciousness will create a fair production and distribution system, which will work efficiently and ensure that all members' needs are met.

The issue to be addressed here is to create an efficient resource allocation system on a large scale, to produce and distribute goods and services equally and fairly.

2) The Pricing System

An accurate information system should be set up to replace the *Price System* of the market economy, in order to establish the *Organic Economy*.

Milton Friedman[9] states that the economic problem may be subdivided into five interrelated problems: fixing standards;

---

[9]   American economist who received the 1976 Nobel Memorial Prize in Economic Sciences.

organizing production; distributing the product; providing for economic maintenance and progress; and adjusting consumption to production over short periods. Prices "do three kinds of things in solving the above five problems. They transmit information, they provide an incentive to users of resources to be guided by this information, and they provide an incentive to owners of resources to follow this information". Then, he adds that "the problem solved by a price system is an extremely complicated one, involving the coordination of the activities of tens and hundreds of millions of people all over the globe and their prompt adjustment to ever-changing conditions. The price system is an extremely subtle and complex device for solving this problem" (Friedman. 2007: 10).

Friedman's focus is about the efficient allocation of resources and economic problems solving, without any consideration of fair or equal distribution of goods and services.

The economic dilemma should not be only about efficient distribution of goods and services, but about how people can meet their needs. Economic systems are not made up of goods and services, but of people who need them. Human values should rule the economic systems to ensure a decent life to all, rather than efficiency rational arguments.

Our objection will be explained by means of an example. Let us suppose that there are ten (10) potential customers and ten (10) products:

- 2 customers can purchase 3 products each; that makes 6 products purchased.

- 4 customers can purchase 1 product each; that makes 4 more products purchased.
- 4 customers can purchase no products; that makes zero (0) additional products purchased, and a total of 10 products.

From an economic perspective, all 10 products were produced and allocated efficiently. But, this system did not allow 40% of consumers to meet their needs of this product.

Another type of system should be created to replace the price system, one that is able to tackle the fair distribution of goods and services, other than the economic problems mentioned above.

3) Coordination and Adjustment

Two key aspects are mentioned by Freeman to solve the economic problems: coordination and adjustment. How can a system be set up to solve the economic problems and deal with the equal distribution issue?

The market economy price system is directly related to the self-interest. Goods and services providers look for adjusting the price to obtain the greatest profit possible without being pushed out from the market by competitors. This way, the self-interest chain spreads throughout the whole system, in order to face a very complex system made up of multiple variables and economic agents simultaneously. But, if we dig a little further, by accepting the price system, we acknowledge our incapacity to create an information system to manage the goods and services production, distribution and purchase. Thus, the market economy system deals only partially with the economic problems.

How can a more equal economic system be created? To do this, the self-interest principle should be replaced with a broadest principle: *the conscious interest.*

4) The "Costs" system

The organic *Costs System*'s guiding principle should be the following: what price should I ask for a good or service that I am providing to myself? The answer will probably be the cost price. Therefore, every conscious individual will offer his service or product at the cost price. *The goods and services price to be offered in an organic economy will be the cost price.*

As per current economic paradigms, the *Costs System* should not be able to provide any company shareholders with the profit required for them to be in the business, or any company with the extra cash needed for increasing their production or make investments. Certainly, under current paradigms this system is not feasible. Our proposal is not to maintain the current system, but to evolve from the market economy system to the organic system, where products and services will be available to all.

Let us suppose that a company needs to make investments to increase its production. From the current economic standpoint, a company will not have enough cash to make investments if products are sold at a cost price. Thus, the company will need to have a profit to make investments in the future. From an organic standpoint, this cash can be included in the cost price. Investments can be included as part of the company's costs.

This seems like the same situation but reversing the events. From an ethical point of view, the organic approach is more justifiable than the first. In the first case, the company is looking to make investments to make profit, based on the self-interest principle. Whereas in the second approach, the company looks for covering its costs, and ensuring there will be enough cash for future investments, to keep on providing the Society with a service.

If there is no profit, why would a company be interested in reducing costs? It is because it should be a matter of consciousness to help as many as possible under the organic paradigm. A company's well-being should include consumers' well-being. It is as if this company is selling to itself or a subsidiary. Likewise, a company should be interested in including technology and increasing productivity in order to benefit all Society members, and to increase its capacity of satisfying more and more consumers, rather than having more cash at its disposal to increase its profit.

Let us make an imaginary mental exercise: A family should be organized so that all members provide others with a good or service. Since all belong to the same family, no member will try to make a profit with the sale of his good or service to the others, but to sell at a cost price to provide them with. This way, any member cares about his family's well-being. Likewise, he will receive products and services from his family members at a cost price as well. Every member will try to provide others with as many goods or services as they need; and they will make their best efforts to increase their productivity, reduce cost, and have good quality. All this for his family's well-being.

This is the main goal of the Organic Economy perspective: *to consider that we all belong to the same family, where the ultimate goal should be to meet all members' needs.*

Thus far, the price system has not been replaced to coordinate and adjust. It only has been redefined as the *Costs System.* For this purpose, the market economy competition concept should be analyzed and potentially replaced with a more cooperative device, likely to be found in an organic structure.

5) Competition

In general, market economic theories establish competition as a way to reduce costs, ensure availability of goods and services, include new technologies and increase productivity, within an illusory scarcity of goods and services.

Producers make up part of a system where the search for profit and competition are supposed to be "natural". This involves practices to increase their market share and harming that of competitors, justified by the self-interest paradigm.

In reality, these kinds of practices are against the harmony of the system, because they induce market instability due to a continuous battle between competitors to maintain/increase their market share, as part of an endless fight with no winners because of the requirements to maintain competition by current legal-economic systems.

If we start from the principle that there is no such scarcity, a different process can be established to reach the same goals, where organic concepts like equality and cooperation can be included.

6) Cooperation

From the organic perspective, producers should be able to constitute a collaborative supply network to provide society with a given product. Each producer should commit to provide quality products, meet demand, and increase productivity for the benefit of Society.

An example will help us explain our point of view: let us assume that ten (10) companies should provide one million (1,000,000) consumers with a specific product. These companies will make up a supply network to meet all consumer's needs, by means of a collaborative process where companies' product price will be *fair*: the cost price. That does not necessarily mean that it will be the same price for all, but that every company will set their price based on their own capital and operations costs: capital investment, production, transport, payroll, sales, distribution, depreciation, etc. They will agree upon which area of the country they will service, share technology improvements, and backup another supplier in case of supply disruption.

As per current paradigms, objections to this system could be the following:

a) **Objection:** Why would a company be interested in producing goods if no profits will be obtained?
   Organic answer: To meet people's needs and provide Society with a service.

b) **Objection:** Since there is no competition, companies will not be interested in improving the product quality, reduce costs, or increase productivity.

    Organic answer: Due to producers' employees' level of consciousness, they will provide Society with the best possible service, including production improvements, productivity increase, and quality of the product.

c) **Objection:** The price difference between products will make the least efficient company go out of the market.

    Organic answer: All ten (10) companies should be seen as production units supplying their correspondent geographical areas, and sharing the same technology. They will sell products at a price to cover their costs. The price differences will be due to internal costs and location factors. Since consumers will be aware of the collaborative relationship between the production units, they will trust the selling price is fair, and thus, will buy their products. No company will go out of the market because all of them will be able to sell their products.

In summary, current economic systems are based on self-interest to shape people's attitudes and way of thinking toward individualistic behaviors. Whereas the organic approach is based on the organic level of consciousness, which makes people consider others as part of himself. This will shape their behavior toward inclusion of others' well-being within their own.

7) The Organic Information system

The flow of information is fundamental in organic structures. Under the current economic perspective, units are classified as producers, distributors, and consumers. But, in the organic approach, production units can be treated as consumers as well, and eventually distributors. Likewise for distributors and consumers, which can be seen as producers as well. The organic approach states that units make up part of a system where there is a *continuous exchange of information and resources.*

An organic structure flow of information is:

- Complete: all units have the comprehensive information for functioning.
- Permanent: there is a continuous flow of information.
- Pertinent: information is useful and applicable to the units' functionality.
- Transitive: information received by one unit is shared with other units.

The ultimate goals of the information system are *coordination* and *adjustment* for the organization of work.

8) Production Information system

A Production Information system will be put in place to know the availability and necessity of goods/services to be produced and distributed, by means of a constant flow of information of citizens' needs on one side, and production inputs needs on the other side.

From a technological point of view, the creation of this type of system should not be an issue. The main questions to answer should be the following:

- How can the needs of citizens be provided in advance?
- How can this information be input into the production system?
- Should this be performed by means of a planning process, or by an online system once products are used?
- How long in advance should the information be input into the system?

A *unit of time* should be defined clearly in the organic information system, so that the production is delivered on a timely manner. The unit of time should be determined by two moments: *beginning*, when the production units receive information of the consumer's needs; and *end*, when the product is produced and actually delivered to the customer.

The information system should have two work paces: *normal condition*, when the information is sent by consumers in a timely manner to the production units at the beginning of the unit of time, and products are delivered within schedule at the end; and *extraordinary conditions*, when the delivery time should be shortened in order to meet exceptional conditions, through a fast track production process.

Under normal conditions, the production process will be as follows:

a) The unit of time is defined per product. This could be one day, one week, one month, etc. It should not be the same for all products, due to the different production process each one of them require.

b) Customer: every customer should provide his needs information per product to the information system at the beginning of the unit of time. If his needs will be the same on a permanent basis, he will not have to provide this information for every single period of time. This request will be renewed automatically unless informed otherwise.

c) Producers: will receive customers' information, plan production, and deliver products at the end of the unit of time.

9) Characteristics of the Information system

Decentralized: there will be as many production units as required to meet demand, scattered throughout various geographical areas. They will be autonomous to plan, produce and meet local quantities requested.

Egalitarian: all citizens will have the same rights to obtain the goods and services they need.

Planned: every member and unit will provide the information system with the input about goods and services they need at the beginning of the process. In the case when this is not possible (i.e. electricity), planning should be performed in advance to estimate the users' needs. This way, production units will be able to plan in advance their product deliveries, including a small surplus in case of any miscalculation, or wrong input.

10) Advantages and Issues to Resolve of the Organic Information system

Advantages

- Information transmission will be accurate and immediately available.

- Production planning will be fluid, and will eliminate the surplus or scarcity of goods and services.
- Distribution of goods will be accurate. This will reduce inventories.
- Products will have the same quality, due to producers being part of the production network and sharing good practices.
- Goods and services will be distributed equally and fairly.
- Production coordination and adjustment will be performed immediately, thanks to the information input at the beginning of the production process.

Issues to resolve

- The information system will not be easy to set up. But it should be feasible due to the current level of information technologies.
- Users should be instructed about how to estimate their needs, and input correctly into the information system.
- Production units should receive inputs, plan their production, and deliver in a timely manner. In the case that one unit is not able to meet its local region demand, support will be provided from the other production units.
- Paradigms should be changed from the current economic system to the organic information system. An adaptation process should be implemented to instruct users and production units about the new system.

A change of modern society paradigms should be performed in order to replace the market economy with an organic economy. This represents a huge hurdle race: overcome current system inertia, break up with market logic tradition, convince people about the benefits of the organic system, and persuade large capitals that this does not present a threat to them.

This type of proposal calls for the people's consciousness. This is addressed to their heart rather than their reason. If people's heart responds to this call, it means that the new economic system is ready to be implemented.

3. ORGANIC COMMUNITIES

> *"Free (or spontaneous) acts are always*
> *phenomena of abundance"*
>
> *Erich Fromm*

Modern societies have been built around urban centers, they are shaped by both the self-interest and bureaucratic-mechanicist paradigms, and most people's life consists of trying to have a job to provide them with enough income to meet their material needs.

But, it may easily be assessed that current economic systems have not guaranteed equal opportunities and same comfort material levels for all, not even in most developed countries. Additionally, their priority is not preserving the environment, which is deemed necessary to ensure the continuity of the system.

The individualist paradigm is opposed to the organic vision of reality; the bureaucratic -mechanicist paradigm does not deal properly with the real sources of motivation of the man, due to not having the flexibility and adaptation characteristics to help organizations survive when facing uncertainty or big changes; and the market economy does not model citizens' conscious of their global reality, nor drive collaborative behaviors among them to reach the general well-being.

A change of paradigms is deemed necessary to create a social order based on harmonious principles, where concepts such as consciousness and collaboration are included. This social order may be established with the right educational system, organizations based on the organic paradigm, and the organic level of consciousness of the majority of the population.

A harmonious social order should be based on organizations that support individuals to meet their material needs, make them work for a common goal, let them perform the best they can, promote their personal and professional development, and encourage collaboration as a way to achieve the general well-being.

In this respect, a proposal should be made to create *organic living communities*, which offer the same level of material comfort as modern societies, but based on collaboration among members to reach the general well-being. Due to the innumerous conflicts existing in big urban centers, our proposal aims to establish communities, where the general well-being can be achieved by means of collaborative behavior, and inter-dependent operation between communities.

Our proposal is based on the creation of *Organic Communities.*

3.1 Precedents

Darib-Drakin (1962) states that communities arise thanks to man's desire for equality and a society based on fairness, freedom and egalitarianism. They do not arise spontaneously, but under exceptional circumstances, urgent needs and revolutionary changes, to get people out of their daily routine and help them overcome their doubts about collective life. This way, pre-historical communities arose, as well as primitive Christian communities, monasteries of the Middle Ages, feudal villages, modern religious communities, utopic socialist communities (i.e. Robert Owen in England, and Charles Fourier in France), Sovietic koljos, Mexican ejido, Chinese peasant communities, and Israelian Kibbutz.

Communities represent a common factor in human history, due to the necessity of interaction and mutual support in social coexistence. Capitalism started displacing communities only 300 years ago, forcing them to exist as isolated groups. Secular communities (i.e. utopic socialist communities) have not lasted as long as religious communities due to the human factor. Religious communities have been organized with people having a common faith and working hard for it; as opposed to socialist communities, where its members were people with no common background or selection criteria. Only the kibbutz, and a few religious communities in North America still exist as examples of community life, based on collective property, production and work, aiming to meet both individual and the community needs.

3.2 Organic Communities

Organic communities are defined as *communities comprised of members who become part of it consciously and voluntarily, with the objectives of providing a way of living based on harmonious principles; offering its members the conditions and means to meet their material, social, and spiritual needs; and having the general well-being as the ultimate goal.*

The *Organic Community* will provide an alternative way of living, different than big urban centers, where the *Conscious Man* can live, study, work, and grow personally-socially-spiritually in an integrated manner to his social environment, within a social order designed to meet his individual needs and achieve the general well-being. The Organic Community will stimulate solidarity and collaboration among people, as part of a harmonious social order.

The Organic Community proposal is based on the principle that the social reality can be modeled as an organic structure. Thus, society can be supported by networked organic communities, rather than big urban centers.

The essential purpose of the Organic Community is meeting the needs of all members, both as individuals and as a part of a community. This can be accomplished as long as members are fully integrated with the community. Individual and collective needs will serve as guidelines for decision-making and actions for every organizational unit.

The individual well-being will include material needs as well as spiritual ones, the latter comprising human interests for any given area, such as art, altruism, contact with nature, volunteerism, consciousness development, friendship, love for others, learning, etc.

All *Organic Communities* will make up part of a network to provide each other with all goods and services they need, to ensure that material, social and spiritual needs are met.

3.3 Organization of Work

All Organic Communities will make up part of a communities network to produce and distribute all goods and services required, as part of a social order where the communities members work will be balanced between their vocation and the community needs.

Traditional bureaucratic production units will be replaced with networked flexible production units (communities) scattered in different geographical areas. Their production planning will be based on the population's needs and their production limitations (i.e. available resources, production capacity, etc.). There will be no chiefs or subordinate employees, but production coordinators and executors, to ensure production goes as planned.

Production coordinators will be selected by their coordination skills, experience, knowledge, and leadership. Their mission will be to "make things happen", not by commanding people, but by facilitating their tasks, including having information available to executors, easing communication between the units, ensuring resources are available, and inviting people to perform their job at a high level of quality.

Every community member will offer his service to the community, and will receive service from others in exchange, be it a good or a service, within an integrated social system where everyone will be able to perform their vocation.

The money circulation will be discouraged and replaced with "equivalent production hours", which will be an equivalent quantity of the socially *necessary work* to be performed by every individual. This way, an equivalent number of hours will be established for every kind of activity within the community. All tasks should be be equally important, but not all of them will require the same number of hours to be accomplished. For example, six (6) working hours in vegetable growing could be equivalent to seven (7) working hours in administration. So, the socially necessary work will depend on the area of work, and the number of hours an individual needs to finish the job.

This approach will be explained with the following example: let us suppose that a given community needs 500 working hours in the vegetable growing area, and 300 working hours in the administration area to run properly. These are the equivalent number of working hours the community needs, which should be performed and assigned to the community members. Initially, the tasks distribution will be done according to people's vocation and the community needs. If not enough members are available to perform a given task, then several members will rotate between their vocation activity and the task the community needs to be performed. This rotation will be done consciously, spontaneously and by mutual agreement between the people involved, to give part of their time usually allocated to their vocation, and replace them with the hours the community needs to fulfill other tasks.

The coordination unit will be of paramount importance, due to the necessity of assigning tasks in a fair manner among the community members. This way, if someone is not pleased with their assigned task, or the amount of hours allocated, he should address the issue with the coordination unit, or directly with the community members.

3.4 Decision-making Processes

Decision-making processes will be based upon what is best for the community. When people's consciousness have reached the organic level, under the right social stimuli and proper social organization, they stop being harmful to their peers and can overcome individualism.

In an organic social order, decisions should be made by consensus. The majority rule has the collateral effect of a losing minority that feels their option for the benefit of the community is not accepted by others. Conflict makes up part of the decision-making process of modern societies, due to the continuous confrontation between different perspectives based on fragmented perceptions of reality. We have the conviction that every decision can be ruled by the principle of what is best for all, to make decisions that lead to the general well-being. If a decision leads to the general well-being, how could it not be made by consensus?

However, sometimes it is not possible to reach a consensus due to various reasons. In this case, a consultation will be made to the "Council of Wise":

> Council of Wise
> The Council of Wise will be a board made up of people well known in the community, recognized by their experience, wisdom and judgment to recommend decisions for the community well-being. They will be elected by consensus. A minimum number of members should be 12 to ensure they represent the diversity of the community.

The community members should be willing to listen to the recommendations from the *Council of Wise* after the consultation, and then make a decision by consensus for the community well-being. If no decision is made by consensus after this consultation, then the majority rule should apply.

3.5 Types of Organic Communities

Every Organic Community will have its own identity and mission, with regards to the products or services they will provide to themselves and other communities. In order to promote the diversity of products and services, each community will have at least one primary product/service that they will offer to other communities, but they can have an array of products or services for their internal use or use of others.

Some communities will focus on farming, others on manufacturing, others on high technology, and so forth. There could even be communities with the mission of research and development, to offer the results of their findings to other communities. All of them making up part of a whole organic system.

The communities' system *organicity* will make possible to replace the market economy, due to the potential interaction and complementation between communities, to buy and sell the products and services they need. The ultimate goal of the general well-being will serve as the guideline to make this possible.

The most important aspects of the *Organic Society* have been highlighted up until now, by means of the organic paradigm concepts application to the organization of work, economic systems, and communities. We will now review the organic paradigm application to the political body of Society: the State. The principles of the *Organic State* will be presented as follows.

CHAPTER 4

THE ORGANIC STATE

There are two different schools of thought regarding the State: the inductive-historical thought represented by Aristotle, Vico, Hegel, Marx and Engels, which expresses that the State is an organizational and political structure that arises from the complexity of the Society, aiming to keep the existing order, and thus, the class system; and, the deductive-logical thought represented by Hobbes, Locke, Kant and Rousseau, which affirms that the State is the political-institutional result of a social contract that allows men to keep order and respect for private property and contracts in exchange of his liberty (Bresser Pereira. 1995).

1. THE STATE AS A STATE OF CONSCIOUSNESS

In ancient times, the State was seen as the best organization of the Society (Plato, Aristotle, and the school of sophists), where individuals and social classes realize the idea of justice as far as possible, giving everyone what is rightfully theirs. During the Middle Age, the discussion was centered on the supremacy of the Church over the State and vice versa, where the first is the spiritual community existing in history, but emerges from this; and the second, is the temporal and historical community. The concept of the State changed radically during the Renaissance, by means of the separation between the State and the Catholic Church as a consequence of the creation of national states, and the reaction to the dominion of the Church. In this regard, the

State is expropriated from its divine foundation and enters the temporality of history.

The State was seen as a pact during the 17th and 18th centuries, either as a contract between men to avoid the struggle of all against all (Hobbes); or as a voluntary renunciation of selfishness coming from the anti-natural state of civilization, and subsequent submission to the general will (Rousseau). Spinoza saw the State as a community of free men, an organization of the Society that grants freedom of thought and religious profession. Kant affirmed that the State is an organization which emerged from a pact and a contract ruled by law, with no regards to the historical origin. The German romantic philosophy identified the State and the Nation as one, where the objective spirit is fully realized, after the opposition between family and civil society has been overcome.

During the 19th century, the discussion about the State debated between individualism and collectivism. Under the first, the State is seen as a balance of the strain between private individual wills. Under the second, this results from eliminating these wills. Marxism regards the State as the dominion of a class. This will disappear through the abolition of classes and achieving the dictatorship of the proletariat.

As can be observed, the concept of the State has changed throughout human history. Man sees the State according to his perception of reality, through the eyeglasses that allow him to define the State according to his concepts, values, and understanding of reality. The State has not been a unique monolithic entity throughout history. If man sees the reality as conflictive, the State will be the balance of these conflicts; if human reality is seen as class struggle, then the State will result from this, and so on. The concept of the State belongs to the man's perception of reality. In other words, *the State will be what the man decides it should be.*

Based on these considerations, we can affirm that the concept of the State results from the man's level of consciousness, rather than its own internal nature. In other words, the essence of the State depends on the man's perception of reality.

2. THE MODERN STATE AND PROCESSES OF CHANGE

The modern state was created as part of the expectations of a society that saw the reality under the modern paradigms. This way, the modern man set up a governmental order based on his interpretation of the Universe: rational, functional, mechanicist, hierarchical, representative and democratic.

Current political and economic paradigms, which shaped the liberal capitalism and market economy, started sometime in the eighteenth century (Polanyi. 1947). They emerged from the modern man's level of consciousness. But these paradigms do not incentivize change of modern institutions, nor the evolution of them. They self-legitimize and establish a totalitarian order on its internal foundations; therefore, refusing the alternatives (Marcuse, 1973).

What if the modern man has already increased his level of consciousness but lives under the same old paradigms? He could be holding fast to concepts, paradigms and institutions which lag behind his unrealized potential organic nature.

Evolution is a common phenomenon that occurs in nature, and man is no different. Consequently, man and his creations, including social institutions and the State, have the natural tendency of evolving, even though current paradigms discourage the change. Admitting that the current social order is basically totalitarian, it has to change as long as man's level of consciousness increases, and the way he sees reality changes. But, how do we know if the general level of consciousness has increased? How can we confirm that current institutions represent a huge burden that must be replaced with lighter ones, more suitable to the new way man is seeing the reality?

One sign may be perceived by the feeling of obsolescence and malfunctioning of a system, showing the necessity for implementing improvements (Kuhn. 1996). Another sign may be the emergence of a paradigm more pertinent to explain the reality, allowing man to better explain facts, or sees it in a more encompassing perspective[10].

If human reality starts to be seen differently, as an organic structure rather than a big machine, then current social, economic and political orders can be questioned. What can lead us to think that the Modern state should be replaced with a different kind of State? A potential answer could be that the paradigms that shaped the Modern State are being replaced with other paradigms, more harmonious, holistic and suitable with the current level of consciousness of man.

Another sign of the Modern State feeling of obsolescence, is the continuous reform projects arising in many countries in order to

---

[10]   As in the case of the Theory of Relativity vs. the Newtonian Theory, where physics phenomena started to be seen and explained differently.

improve it. Proposals are frequently made to reform the functions and organization of Modern States to better respond to the society expectations.

In order to achieve better results and overcome the feeling of obsolescence, it is deemed necessary to set up a different approach to reformulate modern public institutions. The State should be seen from a different point of view. The *organic perspective* may be an answer.

Starting from the fact that organizations can be seen as organic structures, and that human behavior may be guided by the organic level of consciousness, it should be possible to design public institutions aligned with more harmonious social paradigms, where both the Society and the State can be shaped under the organic perspective.

3. THE ORGANIC STATE

The Society and the State can be seen as organic structures under the organic perspective. The State can be shaped as an organic unit with well-defined duties within the *organic society*, such as the following:

a) Provide the necessary conditions to all organic units to fulfill their tasks.

b) Intervene when required to solve an issue that prevents any given organic units from fulfilling their tasks, or interacting freely and fairly.

The main duty of the State should be to ensure that the whole system operates properly. It should act as the *general coordination* unit. In this sense, the Organic State will make certain that all other units perform well. It will not be the main unit, or the driver of the economic system, but the support provider to the rest of the units. The State will accompany the natural development of the social structures, provide support to the economic units, coordinate the proper operation of the system, and give assistance to every unit to fulfill their task.

The Organic State will continuously monitor the operation of the Organic Society, and will make sure everything works as expected. Figure 4.1 below shows the Organic Society structure, the Organic State, and two given units A and B, which will receive the support from the State in case of disruption of the resources that should be received, or the required information to perform their tasks.

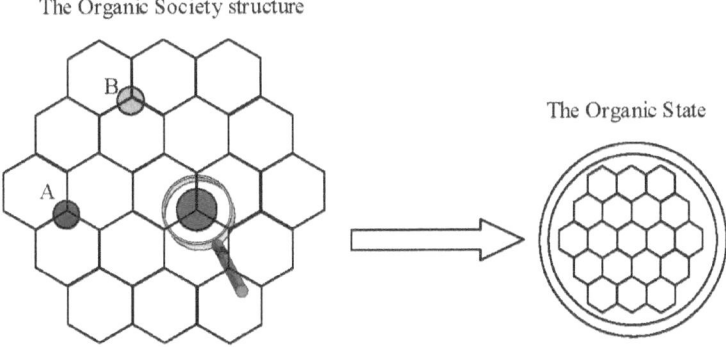

Fig. 4.1: The Organic Society and the Organic State

As stated above, the Organic State will serve as the general coordination unit within the Organic Society, to ensure that the rest of units interact freely and fairly to fulfill their tasks and accomplish their mission.

As inferred from the figure above, the State will be internally organized as an organic structure, with a coordination unit and units that should fulfill their tasks within its own internal framework.

4. THE EVOLVEMENT FROM THE MODERN STATE TO THE ORGANIC STATE

The evolvement from the Modern State to the Organic State should be implemented in three clearly different stages, where the State will be modifying both its functions and its structure.

4.1 First Stage

The State will assume the organic paradigm as a guideline to implement its transformation. This will include measures intended to modify its structure, functionality, and its role within the social order.

In order to put the organic social order in place, the State should intermediate between all parts, coordinate the process, and provide the conditions that will lead to the establishment of the Organic Society, including the social and economic institutions that will make part of it. Providing these conditions will include the following:

- Establishing a legal system where the organic principles will be set up as an alternative of the social order.

- Implementing public policies to create the Organic Communities.
- Setting up a network informational system to allow the free flow of information, knowledge, resources, services and goods between all sectors of the society, including economic and social units.
- Delegating progressively some responsibilities from the State to Organic Communities, like elementary education and ambulatory health care.
- Creating educational and awareness programs of the organic paradigm.

This process will be held under the organic perspective. That is, the State will assume an organic behavior to tackle this process: hierarchy will be replaced with coordination, and leadership will be in every unit making up part of the transition. The State will not assume a hierarchical authority that will decide "from top to bottom", or have control over the process, but will coordinate and ensure that all conditions are met to put it in place and make it work.

The State will promote the assimilation of its new organic identity, where decentralization, autonomy, flexibility and network will shape its function. The following measures are recommended for this:

a) Federal government institutions will be created in every state or province to promote a real decentralization by means of the creation of "mini-agencies", and remove the traditional bureaucratic centralized institution. Every state/province institution will harmonize their public policies with other states/provinces units. The former federal institution will coordinate rather than implement and make it work.

b) Hierarchical relationships will be replaced with coordination and interaction between all public administration units, to encourage teamwork and networking. Flexibility, interaction, and implicate order leadership will shape its operation.

4.2 Maintenance of Order and Respect of Contracts

Maintenance of order and respect of contracts will depend on the level of consciousness of every individual and the system's organicity rather than on enforcement procedures, be it repression or social pressure to adopt a given organic behavior.

Repression works when an individual respects the law due to the fear of being punished, even when he may not end up being punished. The enforcement of the law for some, represents a coercion effect over the rest of the population. This coercion effect works when existing on a small scale: theft, corruption or traffic offenses can be controlled when they represent a small number compared to the size of the population. A high proportion of the population will probably not suffer from the repression from the State themselves, but they will repress themselves from committing any offense against the law by seeing it enforced on others. But, if offenses are committed on a large scale, the repressive function of the State can be overtaken, and not all offenders would be punished.

The capacity of the modern State to ensure that order is maintained and contracts are respected is based on its *dissuasion capacity* rather than its ability to deal with them at a large scale. It can work when only a small proportion of the population does not respect order or contracts. But, should the majority of the population disregard the existing order, the State would be incapable of fulfilling this responsibility. If this happens, the State's duty to ensure that order is maintained and contracts are respected may not even be legitimate, due to the democratic rule of the majority. Should the majority decide not to maintain order and respect contracts, the State would have to abide by this rule.

But, we do not want to go that far and question the existence of a Society ruled by the order and respect of contracts. We only want to highlight the following statement: *if the majority decides to maintain order and respect contracts willingly, based on their organic level of consciousness rather than by the State's enforcement of the law, then the State should respect this mandate and delegate this duty to every individual and the community they live in.*

This statement affirms that what really compels someone to behave a given way is within him rather than due to the external conditions, even when the same apparent result can be achieved. The State makes up part of the external conditions, but these conditions really come from the internal level of consciousness of people. The State is the expression of the majority will. If the majority wants the State to maintain order and make contracts be respected, then the State will have to do so. The State exists due to the people and should govern for them, without any sort of own free will. It justifies its existence as long as it fulfills a need people cannot fulfill by themselves. But, if order is maintained and contracts are respected spontaneously thanks to the people's level of consciousness and mutual respect, then the State would have to delegate both tasks to the people.

The majority of people, if not all, will wish to maintain order and respect contracts in an *Organic Society*, due their organic level of consciousness, which will conduct their behavior and relationships with others. Additionally, all political, social, and economical institutions will be shaped by this level of consciousness. Therefore, there should not be the need of enforcement by the State.

4.3 Second Stage

On the second stage, the State will transfer part of its responsibilities to the new organic institutions that will emerge as part of the organic arrangement. Its traditional role of leading and intervening will be replaced with coordinating and ensuring organic processes happen, while being discharged from administrative functions that can be performed by organic institutions.

The State will be responsible for the following tasks during this second stage:

a) <u>Executive level:</u> the State should be responsible to ensure that all conditions are met for all units to fulfill their responsibilities, intervene when required to resolve an issue that impedes the spontaneous interaction between two (2) given organic units, and coordinate the progressive implementation of the Organic Society structure, in conjunction with other actors participating in the process (i.e. political institutions, universities, NGOs, organic communities, scientific and religious groups, etc.).

b) <u>Legislative level:</u> the legal structure will be based on the **Law of Love** and the organic level of consciousness, to encourage harmony in the social order, promote the personal growth of individuals, expand prosperity to all, and encourage respect for people, cultural expressions and the environment. The acceptance of the *Law of Love* will inspire the rest of the laws that will rule the Organic Society to stimulate the peaceful cohabitation among people, accepting the Society as a common goal, acknowledging that we all make part of the same species, and assuming the responsibility of taking care of our own beautiful planet. The legal rearrangement of the Society will start by accepting that the *Law of Love* should guide our lives, our relationship with others, the design of our social-political-economical institutions, and the world order. This will allow the human species to recognize itself as an indivisible whole, essentially harmonious, and respectful towards people's individuality, the social order, and the environment. The Organic Society and its institutions will adapt their structure and functions to secure the compliance with the *fundamental law.*

c) <u>Political level:</u> the State and the Society will define together the means by which the decisions will be made, citizens will communicate their opinions and expectations, and how they will participate in the social realm. Communication will be interactive and intensive between all participants of the Society to shape the Organic Society.

d) <u>Judiciary level:</u> since people will behave according to the organic level of consciousness, a traditional law enforcement system will not be necessary to ensure that rules and norms are respected. The primary law enforcer will be the level of consciousness of the people, to make sure that they *enforce* the **Law of Love** by themselves. In the case of someone acting against the supreme law, the real punishment will come from inside, due to the regrets of having acted against others, and ultimately against himself. If someone if not aware of his law infringement, others will try to show him the consequences of his actions. When an individual acts against the Society, he must understand that he is acting against others and against himself, and should try to correct his error. The State will be part of this process but only at a second stage, to show any given individual the consequences of his actions against the social harmony if he does not realize this.

4.4 Third Stage

On the third stage, the State will no longer be a monolithic institution, but an integrated agency within the organic structure, scattered demographically and by areas of participation. Its main duty will be to coordinate the interactions between the organic communities, and monitor their functions. It will be made up of *State Organic units* embedded into the society organic structure to ensure the system runs properly (see figure below). The state will be each one and all of them at the same time, thus, assuming the autopoietic property of the organic structure. Its main function will be to ensure that conditions are met for Organic communities to perform their duties, rather than performing them by itself.

As stated above, the *Organic State* will be the set of all mini-States embedded in the structure and each one of them, with the duty of coordinating and monitoring the Organic Society. The State will be an organic structure within the Organic Society.

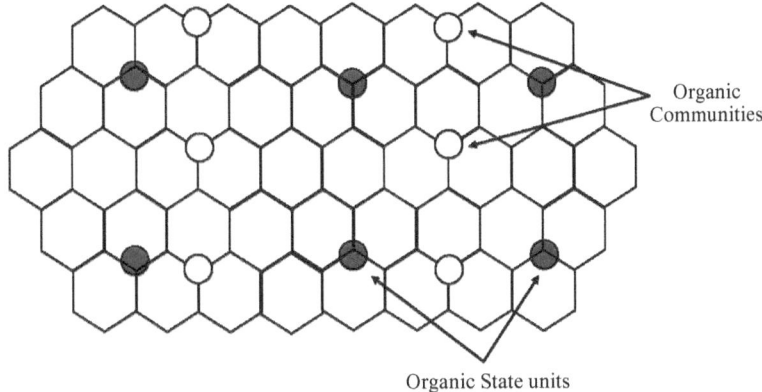

Fig. 4.2: The Organic Society and the Organic State

Every State Unit will have the function of coordinating and monitoring the Organic Communities within its geographical range. Since the Organic State will be every unit and all units at the same time, its graphic representation will be as follows:

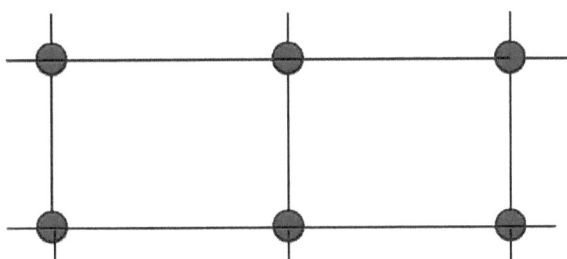

Fig 4.3: The Organic state

The Organic State will be comprised of the *State Organic Communities* existing in the Organic Society, interconnected with each other by means of a network that will allow the right and timely flow of information, resources and people. Every community will have the characteristics of the atomized and holographic organization:

based on teams, decentralized, autonomous, redundant, differentiated by objectives and geographical area, and integrated by intensive communications (Motta. 1991).

Many responsibilities currently fulfilled by the Modern State will be performed by the Organic Communities, or by the citizens, among which are the following:

- Health: every Organic Community can provide general medical services at a local level through ambulatory care. For more sophisticated or specialized health services, there will be a Health Organic Community for a given geographical area.
- Security: an Organic Society, made up of conscious citizens working for their own and the general well-being, will not need an enforcement agency to ensure the law is respected. Enforcement tasks will tend to disappear as long as the general consciousness level rises, and will be replaced with crime prevention strategies within and outside every Organic Community.
- Public Services: some public services can be provided by the Organic Communities to their population (i.e. emergency medical services, postal service, libraries, etc.). Other public services should still be provided by the Organic State (i.e. transportation, electricity, gas, large health care facilities, military, etc.). In the case of waste management, it can be provided by both the Organic Communities and the Organic State.
- Education: every Organic Community can provide education until a certain level (i.e. elementary, high school, etc.).

Undergraduate education and above can be provided by colleges/universities, which can still be separate entities, or structured as Organic Communities.

- Defense: military expenditures will be reduced and defense against foreign countries will tend to disappear as long as the organic paradigm is internationally accepted, by assuming that we all make up part of the same race, that we inhabit one planet, and that we all share a common fate.

- International relations: borders between countries will tend to disappear until a point where a World Government will be created, and countries will become provinces or states making up part of this government. Every human being will be represented by this government, without any sort of distinction based on race, religion, or origin. International relations will be replaced with "Inter-provincial relations", to ensure the right flow of information, communication, and interaction between any given provinces, states, regions or organic communities of the world.

- Legal basis: the **Law of Love** will be the basis of the Organic Society legal system, and will inspire all norms and contracts that will rule the social realm. Even that laws can still be created by legislatives bodies, it will not be an exclusive duty of them to interpret or enforce the *Law of Love*. Love is in every child, every person, every social group, every natural scenery, and every manifestation of the Creation. This should not only be taught in schools, or be ruled by government bodies. Love is a universal force that can rule our behavior and social integration. Love gives meaning to our lives, feeds us, moves us, makes us fall in *love*, delights us, protects us, teaches us, shows us the path to follow, and where we should be. Human beings will be pleased by acting by the Law of Love, which will show us mutual giving, servicing others, support and respect for others and oneself. Therefore, do we need to implement laws different than the Law of Love to set up the legal basis of the Organic Society? Only in the case they are subject to the fundamental law. The Law of Love should be the supreme norm, and other laws should be based on it. Love does not have to be enforced by any agency. It exists and it is real. But, we need to accept it as a fundamental part of our human essence, and implement the proper incentives to base every human manifestation on it.

The State will no longer be as it exists today: a bureaucratic structure ruling the society, but it will be an active participant within the organic social structure. The State will provide support to the organic communities and the society in general, to help them run properly.

The next chapter will be about processes of change in organic systems, and how they can be applied at organizational and social levels.

CHAPTER 5

PROCESSES OF CHANGE

A few concepts will be reviewed with regards to processes of change, in order to have a better understanding of the transition that could lead from the current order to the establishment of the *Organic Society*.

1. THE EXTERNAL AS A MANIFESTATION OF THE INTERNAL

The external is the manifestation of the internal. All that exists is the materialization of people's thoughts, and ultimately, their level of consciousness. No change is possible unless an internal change occurs in how people see the reality.

In addition to that, every person sees and interprets the reality according to his own internal world. Man sees the reality in a way that he can understand it. The 19th century man saw the Universe as a big clock, an enormous system that worked under the same principles as the machines he was able to design and build. The 20th century man sees the Universe under the Einsteinian relativistic principle, where the quantum physics discoveries showed a sub-atomic universe beyond our *Newtonian* comprehension. A different language had to be created to understand the atomic laws and interpret what was being revealed.

Based on his values, knowledge, experience, intuition and consciousness, man interprets the surrounding reality based on what he sees, and perceives what he is able to understand. In this sense, a mystic man will see a mystic reality, a religious man will see a religious reality, a rational man will perceive a rational reality, and a conscious man will see a conscious reality.

2. CHANGES OCCUR FROM WITHIN OUTWARDS

Throughout human history, many changes occurred when the majority of the people understood that it was not possible to continue with the current system, and decided to either change the system, or replace it with a different one. These kinds of changes, like the French Revolution, the Bolshevik Revolution or the fall of the Berlin Wall, did not occur as an initiative of the State, *from top to bottom,* precisely because this is one of the institutions that needed to be changed; nor did they occur as an exclusive initiative of the people, *from bottom to top,* because they are not powerful enough to do it by themselves. But, they occurred *from within outwards.*

These kinds of changes occurred when the whole society perceived that it was no longer possible to continue with the existing order, that this order was unsustainable, and that it had to be changed radically in a short period of time. Suddenly, the society realized that this order had to be replaced with a new type of order, and a big step forward had to be taken into the future. Subsequent events came due to a change in the people's *level of consciousness*, showing a change in their internal understanding of the social reality, and the want to voice it openly. Thus, generated a shift *from within outwards.*

However, this change in the level of consciousness on a few people was not enough to induce a change on a large scale, no matter if it made sense, or if these people had the power to implement it. It was necessary a change in the level of consciousness in many people, so that perceptible changes in the existing social order could be implemented.

Therefore, it is necessary to increase the level of consciousness on a sufficient number of people in order to change the status quo. As stated above, a real transformation in the existing order *does not come from top to bottom or bottom to top, but from within outwards.*

3. PRINCIPLES OF CHANGE AND CRITICAL MASS

3.1 Principles of Change

a) The Minimalist Principle

This principle states that any change should be implemented by means of small steps towards the desired goal, in order to nullify the natural inertia of every single step. The *Minimalist Principle* is based on recognizing that there are natural opposing forces to any action exerted on a different direction than the reality momentum. It is necessary to proceed gradually towards the desired direction in order to achieve a given goal, step by step and not drastically, to reduce the risk of the opposite effect that may arise due to the existing reaction force to any exerted action[11].

The Minimalist Principle is fully incorporated in eastern cultures. Every idea and every action are executed gradually, in order to nullify the opposing force that exists in every step. Eastern cultures treat

---

[11]   The law of action-reaction (Newton's third law) explains that the force exerted by one object upon a second object is equal in magnitude and opposite direction to the force exerted by the second object upon the first object.

the ideas as plants that need to grow and flourish. If someone has an idea, he will not shout it with all his force, but place it in reserve to give it time to mature. This time of reflection, or decantation, gives the opportunity to nullify all opposing forces, and advance towards the desired destination.

b) Radical Action

However, sometimes it is not possible to reach a given desired state only by acting through the Minimalist Principle, either because obstacles are bigger than expected, or because there is not enough time to let the situation mature fully, or especially, because the Minimalist Principle has paved the way to exert a more radical action. In any of these cases, an intensified effort should be executed. This is what is called a *Radical Action*, which can be defined as a *drastic action, usually stronger than a minimalistic action, with the objective of providing a decisive momentum to drive circumstances towards the desired result.*

Every Radical Action has secondary effects, and it will take some time before a *state of equilibrium* is reached, where all of these effects will recede and reach a state where all opposing forces will be nullified or integrated to the natural inertia towards to the desired state.

It should be mentioned that a Radical Action should be within certain limits, not bigger than required, in order to prevent the *Pendulum Effect* from happening.

c) The Pendulum Effect

The Pendulum Effect happens when the Radical Action is so strong, higher than the desired level, that *the magnitude of the reaction force will generate the opposing effect,* making circumstances go backwards to a point behind where the Radical Action was exerted. From that moment on, circumstances will turn into a *back and forth* movement like a pendulum, until they reach a new equilibrium.

This final equilibrium could be ahead of the starting equilibrium point. That is, towards the direction where the Radical Action was exerted. But this will not be necessarily the case, due to "hidden" forces, or not foreseen at the starting point. This can make that the new equilibrium be behind the starting point, or in another direction. In any case, a new equilibrium will be attained after this strong Radical Action is exerted and the *Pendulum Effect* movement ceases.

In the case where the *Pendulum Effect* makes circumstances move towards the desired direction, the new equilibrium will be close to where it was expected, once the back and forth movement is over, due to end of the reaction force and collateral effects.

Graphically, the *Pendulum Effect* is shown as follows:

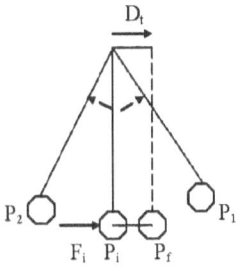

P_i: Initial situation (original equilibrium)
F_i: Initial force (Radical Action)
P_1: Point where the back and force movement starts
P_2: Point where the movement starts to be in the same direction as the Radical Action
P_f: Final situation (new equilibrium)
D_t: Total "distance"

Fig. 5.1: Pendulum Effect

The above mentioned principles (Minimalist Principle, Radical Action, and Pendulum Effect) are applicable to different kinds of organic systems (i.e. social, organizational, etc.).

Critical Mass

The concept of *Critical Mass* refers to *a sufficient number of people capable of inducing transformations on a given social system.*

The implementation of social changes aiming at the establishment of the *Organic Society* may come through an awareness-raising process, where a number of people equivalent or greater than the *critical mass* can induce transformations in that direction.

Once this awareness-raising process occurs, various scenarios may happen. One could be the purposeful implementation of *minimalistic actions* on educational systems, private and public organizations, political order, legal framework and economic systems at a global level, to pave the way for exerting a Radical Action to establish the Organic Society. Another scenario could be the execution of a Radical Plan to establish the Organic Society in a short period of time, assuming the risks of the side effects that may occur, by means of establishing the **Law of Love** worldwide as the base for setting up any social/organizational system, and make progressive adjustments at organizational, institutional, political, legal and economic levels, as issues arise.

No matter what process is chosen, this change will impact the way people see the reality, by means of increasing their level of consciousness, and *implementing changes from within outwards.*

As for the critical mass, there is not an accurate count of people that can be provided in order to induce this type of transformations in the society. This will be recognized when it comes, due to the winds of change that will arise at all levels, externalizing a *general sensation that the existing order should be replaced*, and showing the necessity of moving ahead.

4. PROCESSES OF CHANGE: GRADUAL PROCESS AND PROCESS VIA CRISIS

4.1 Gradual Change

A gradual process leading to the creation of the *Organic Society,* should be comprised of intermediary processes to make the organic paradigm part of social institutions. Achieving the critical mass of people who want and work for these processes to happen is of paramount importance. Once the critical mass of people is achieved, then a plan can be put in place to advance in that direction.

This plan should include *minimalistic actions* intended to reach the general well-being by increasing the general level of consciousness of people, showing the people the feasibility of living in a more collaborative way and with more solidarity, and assimilating the convenience of replacing current conflictive paradigms with the organic paradigm. There should be educational programs, seminars, private companies' workshops, government institutions programs, and articles in newspapers/magazines showing the necessity of rearranging the society under the organic paradigm. There will certainly be other kind of minimalistic actions that we cannot foresee at the moment, which may be proposed by people being part of the critical mass with the same expectations of establishing the Organic Society, but they will provide support to reach the same goal.

The time will come when a *Radical Action* can be exerted, where minimalistic actions will have paved the way to transform the *organic movement* into a mass movement of people trying to live in a more peaceful and harmonious way, where all people's necessities will be worthy of being met, and our planet will be widely respected. This Radical Action could be the establishment of Organic Communities at a large scale, or a political party that will work for implementing the organic paradigm, or the creation of a network of people living under the organic paradigm. This Radical Action will show the aspiration of an important sector of society to live under the organic paradigm.

All those who want to live under the organic paradigm should be careful enough to avoid exerting a Radical Action too strong, in order to prevent the emergence of opposing forces bigger than expected, which may generate the undesirable *Pendulum Effect,* and not risk going back to a situation before where the minimalistic actions started being exerted. If this happens, the achievements made through all minimalistic actions may disappear. Caution and restraint should guide every single action leading to the establishment of the organic paradigm as part of the social order.

Once all minimalistic actions and specific Radical Actions have been made rightly, it will be only a matter of time until the emergence of the *Organic Society,* where concepts such as Love, harmony, collaboration and solidarity will make up part of communities, organizations and the social order.

4.2 Change via Crisis

Current social paradigms are mostly mechanistic and rationalistic. But, if the society starts to be seen as an organic system and social paradigms start being adopted, at some point in the future it will turn into an Organic Society. The only thing that is permanent in human history is the change of paradigms and social structures. Human reality keeps changing over time, in a continuous sequence of states of equilibrium and transition processes, always towards *higher complexity states of equilibrium*[12].

On the other hand, if Modern Society is seen as a state of equilibrium in human history, it may be assumed that a transition process will come at a certain moment in the future, where a higher complexity and more diversified state of equilibrium result. Thus, a change will inevitably come in the natural process of the social order evolution.

This change may come under one of the following processes:

a) *A continuous and incremental way*, where changes come as part of an intended process of minimalistic actions and specific radical actions to set up a more evolved social order.
b) Via *crisis* of the current order, where drastic changes may arise as a result of man's intention to prevent changes from happening, that may induce chaotic events due to not letting circumstances follow the natural flow of evolution.

---

[12] Non-equilibrium may become a source of order in processes of thermodynamic systems, and evolution towards more complex and diversified systems (Nicolis and Prigogine, 1977).

The downside of "choosing" the *crisis* option, either because man is not capable of implementing the required changes, or because the people in charge do not want to do it in order to keep their benefits, is that the change process might be chaotic, less organized, have violent demonstrations and unpredictable results.

Permitting a change process via *crisis* opens the possibility of undesirable situations: instability, violence, institutional inoperability, incapability of maintaining order, and fear of uncertainty. Fear is the worst of the motivational drivers, because it creates feelings of anxiety, which inhibits the ability of making sound and well-considered decisions. Fear at a large scale may unleash the phenomenon of mass hysteria, which would have disastrous consequences to current political, economic, and social systems.

A change via *crisis* opens up the possibility of spontaneous self-organization, just like thermodynamic systems (Nicolis and Prigogine, 1977), where a collaborative social order may surface, due to the hardships caused by the scarcity of resources, goods, and food, which may induce the creation of organizations and social institutions shaped by the organic paradigm for the survival of the system.

In any case, the risks associated with a change via *crisis* are high enough to make us work for *continuous and incremental* changes of current economic, political, and social orders towards a more harmonious society.

The item in discussion is not whether the change will happen or not, but when and how it is going to happen. Change is part of the social nature of man, and the implementation of changes to establish a more collaborative and supportive system makes up part of the natural evolution of mankind, and the expectations of millions of people desiring to live in a more harmonious, integrated, and collaborative way.

The Modern Society should be seen as starting point of new theoretical possibilities of social organization, rather than a point of arrival. Same as the two big scientific revolutions of the 20th century: *Relativity*, which meant the end of universality; and *Quantum Mechanics*, which implied the end of materialism (Nicolis and Prigogine, 1977). The higher our capability of implementing social and organizational changes in a smooth and natural manner, the higher the probabilities of sailing through the deep waters of the natural flow of evolution with no big setbacks.

CONCLUSION

"Ideals are like stars: you will not succeed in touching them,
But following them you will reach your destiny"

Carl Schurz

The history of mankind shows the necessity of making one step further to base the social order on different paradigms than current ones. A major step ahead should be made by man to build a better future for humankind. Love, harmony, collaboration and solidarity must be included in the speech of global changes to be implemented at organizational and social levels. The rational paradigm has paved the way to include new sources of inspiration in the human evolution process. A new paradigm should be set up to let free our imagination, and believe in a future where *Love* shows the window of possibilities, which are becoming more real, of transforming the organizational and social realities into catalysts of collaboration and caring among people.

We must go out to meet new possibilities to bring the spiritual world perfection to the material world. The most sublime human manifestations should be brought to the real world, in order to dream of a better future for humankind. The human social evolution should be based on the consciousness of being part of an intrinsically wonderful and harmonious natural order, and must be the benchmark of upcoming organizational and social institutions representations.

Mother Nature has provided us with a set of conditions to stimulate the human development. The time has now come for man to become the creator of a harmonious reality that will shape social and organizational institutions, as well as his relationship with the natural environment. The time has come for man to have a symbiotic relationship with social and natural orders. The dichotomy between man and man, or between man and nature cannot continue. The universal order shows the possibility of considering the reality as a harmoniously integrated whole, and essentially caring. The time has come for man to recognize the necessity of modeling his relationships with others and with nature based on the *Law of Love*.

The *Law of Love* and the creation of the *Organic Society* show what can be done at both organizational and social levels. When man wakes up and listens to his Heart, he will be capable of designing a social order where the *separateness* can be finally overcome. The organic structure is a powerful tool to stimulate man's integration to both society and nature, more powerful than the existing individualistic and rational paradigms.

There might be other proposals aiming to explore the right way of man to collaborate and organize into communities. We welcome any proposal aiming to overcome the existing *separateness* of modern man, and support any initiative aiming to develop collaboration and solidarity among people, as a way to shape the social order. At the moment, this is our proposal: the assumption of the *Law of Love* and the establishment of *The Organic Society*, which came as a result of a deep reflection about the different possibilities the man may choose in the course of his evolution.

REFERENCES

Bertalanffy, Ludwig Von. *General System Theory.* New York. Braziller, 1969.

Bohm, David. *Wholeness and the Implicate Order.* Routledge. London and New York, 2002.

Boulding, Kenneth. *The Organizational Revolution.* Harper Brothers. NY, 1953.

Bresser Pereira, Luiz Carlos. *Estado, Aparelho de Estado e Sociedade Civil.* ENAP/MARE. Brasília, 1995.

Darin-Drabkin, H. *La Otra Sociedad.* Fondo de Cultura Económica. México, 1962.

Drèze, Jean e Sen, Amartya. *The Political Economy of Hunger- Vol. 1.* Clarendon Press. Oxford, 1990.

Friedman, Milton. *Price Theory.* Transaction Publishers. New Brunswick, New Jersey, 2007.

Fromm, Erich. *The Fear of Freedom.* http://realsociology.edublogs.org/files/2013/09/erich-fromm-the-fear-of-freedom-escape-from-freedom-29wevxr.pdf. Great Britan, 1942. Accessed 2016.

_____. *El Miedo a la Libertad.* Abril. Buenos Aires, 1952.

Gandhi, Mahatma. *All Men Are Brothers.* Unesco. Paris, 1958.

Gomes Penna, Antônio. *Sobre as Teorias Sociais da Consciência.* Arquivos Brasileiros de Psicologia. FGV. Rio de Janeiro, Jan/Mar 1985.

Hobbes, Thomas. *Leviatan.* Fondo de Cultura Econômica. México, 1940.

Kuhn, Thomas. *A Estrutura das Revoluções Científicas.* Perspectiva. São Paulo, 1996.

Jung, Carl. *El Yo y el Inconsciente.* Miracle. Barcelona, 1955.

_____. *Carl Jung Resources > Quotes.* http://www.carl-jung.net/quotes.html#collectiveuncnsc. Accessed 2016.

Leite, José Eduardo Teixeira. *Nós Quem, Cara Pálida? A razão depois de Taylor* In *Recursos Humanos e Subjetividade.* Vozes. Petrópolis, 1995.

Locke, John. *Segundo Tratado sobre o Governo.* Ibrasa. São Paulo, 1963.

Marcuse, Hebert. *A Ideologia da Sociedade Industrial: O Homem Unidimensional.* Rio de Janeiro. Zahar, 1973.

Maslow, Abraham. *Motivación y Personalidad.* Sagitario. Barcelona, 1963.

Maturana, Humberto and Varela, Francisco. *Autopoiesis and Cognition -The Realization of the Living.* Reidel. Durdrecht-Holland, 1980.

_____. *Autopoiesis and Cognition -The Realization of the Living.* https://books.google.ca/books?id=nVmcN9Ja68kC&pg=PA13&redir_esc=y#v=onepage&q&f=false. Accessed 2016.

Motta, Paulo Roberto. *A Ciência e Arte de Ser Dirigente.* Record. Rio de Janeiro, 1991.

Murray, Edward. *Motivação e Emoção.* Zahar. Rio de Janeiro, 1967.

Nicolis, G. and Prigogine, I. *Self-Organization in Nonequilibrium Systems - from dissipative structures to order through fluctuations.* Wiley-Interscience. New York, 1977.

Poincaré, Henri. *A Ciência e a Hipótese.* Editora UnB. Brasília, 1984 (Publicado em 1902).

Polanyi, Karl. *On belief in Economic Determinism.* Sociological Review, vol. a39, Issue 1, January 1947.

Rousseau, Jean-Jacques. *Contrato Social.* Organização Simões. Rio de Janeiro, 1951 (1762).

Skinner, B. F. *Walden II – Uma Sociedade do Futuro.* Editora Pedagógica e Universitária. São Paulo, 1977.